THE BOOK IN A BOX METHOD

THE **GROUNDBREAKING** NEW WAY
TO WRITE AND PUBLISH **YOUR BOOK**

THE

BOOK

—— IN A ——

BOX

METHOD

#1 NEW YORK TIMES BESTSELLING AUTHOR
TUCKER MAX
—— and ——
ZACH OBRONT

THE BOOK IN A BOX METHOD
*The Groundbreaking New Way
to Write and Publish Your Book*

ISBN   978-1-61961-346-1   *Print*
        978-1-61961-347-8   *Ebook*

This book is for everyone
who has a great book
in them, but doesn't
know how to get it out.

CONTENTS

INTRODUCTION

At first, it sounded like a ridiculous question:

"I want to write a book, but I don't have the time, and the publishing process is so confusing and frustrating. How can I get my ideas into a book without having to deal with all of this?"

Even though I'd been writing books for over a decade, I didn't know how to answer. So I did what most people do when faced with an uncomfortable situation that makes them question their identity and all their long-held assumptions—I turned it back on the questioner and used snark to shame her:

"Are you asking me how you can write a book...without writing it?"

Yes, she nodded.

I chuckled at her, arrogantly explained "how writing actually works," and proceeded to give her a condescending lesson in literary history. I sounded exactly like one of those snobbish articles that I would usually make fun of, where a "serious" writer decries the ills of blogging. I even went so far as to question her work ethic.

This was extremely rich, as this woman, Melissa Gonzalez, had probably accomplished more in the last year than I had in ten. She started and ran a very successful pop-up retail company and wanted to write a book only because so many people had asked her to share her wisdom with them. The only reason she didn't have time to think about publishing was because she was too busy running successful pop-ups.

After enduring my elitist nonsense for long enough, she dropped the bomb that would not only (rightfully) devastate my ego, but also launch this book (and a company):

"You're an entrepreneur, right? Isn't an entrepreneur someone who solves problems? Are you going to help me solve my problem, or just lecture me about hard work?"

Boom.

THE DEVELOPMENT OF THE SOLUTION

Because of that conversation—and my shame at being such an elitist hypocrite—my co-founder (Zach Obront) and I developed an entirely new way to create a high-quality, professional book.

We called it the "Book In A Box" process, and it worked incredibly well for Melissa. Here's we did it:

First, we helped her understand her goals for the book, who she wanted the book to reach, and what ideas and stories she wanted to include to reach that audience. This gave us the book positioning and structure for the outline and content of the book.

Once we'd structured that content into an outline, we spent about twelve hours on the phone interviewing her (broken into several small sessions), and got everything she knew about pop-up retail out of her head and onto an audio recording. All of the things she'd learned in a decade of pioneering this niche industry, she shared with and explained to us.

We then took the audio recording of these interviews and had them transcribed. We took that transcription and essentially "translated" it in pretty good manuscript. It was her ideas, her words and her voice.

We then worked with her to edit the manuscript so that it perfectly reflected her ideas and voice.

We did all of the rest of the publishing work (cover design, interior design, distribution, etc.), and launched her book five months later.

Since then, the book has:

1. Allowed her to share all of her ideas and knowledge with all of the people who couldn't afford her services.

2. Landed her multi-million dollar consulting contracts with major national retailers.

3. Led to her doing three keynote speeches at major retail conferences.

4. Tripled the incoming business to her company.

In all ways, this book was a huge success for Melissa.

We quickly realized that the process we used was much bigger than just one book. This was because Melissa's problem was not unique at all. In fact, we had dozens of people coming to us to get the same service *before we even had a website selling it.*

When you're selling something before you even have a company set up to offer it, you know you've discovered a real problem that a lot of people want to solve.

THE SOLUTION SOLVES A BIGGER PROBLEM

There are thousands of people just like Melissa: knowledgeable, accomplished professionals who have great books locked up in their heads, and aren't writing them only because the process of writing a book is too time-consuming and difficult.

Think about it. How many brilliant people do you know who should have a book, and don't? Quite a few, I bet. As their friend, you get to hear their wisdom and learn from it, but what about the rest of the people who could benefit from their knowledge? They are out of luck.

You're probably reading this because *you know there's possibly an important book in your head*, and people have asked you to share it...but you haven't written it.

Yet.

WHY HAVEN'T YOU WRITTEN YOUR BOOK?

So why not? Why haven't you written that book?

Because you ran into the same problem that Melissa did:

The conventional process for writing a book doesn't work for people who don't have time to dedicate their entire life to doing it.

Here are the basic steps required to write a book:

1. Figure out exactly what your book is about.

2. Figure out exactly how to structure the book so it'll make sense to the reader.

3. Find a quiet place you can concentrate while you write.

4. Find several hours a day of free time to write so you can write your book.

5. If you aren't already, give yourself enough time to become a good enough writer so you can actually convey your wisdom properly in the book.

6. Then, even if you can do all of that and finish your book, you still have to figure out how the hell to publish the book, which is a lot of work.

This is a ridiculous amount of work, even if you don't already have a full time profession and life.

So what happens? The book never gets done. And you never share your wisdom, and the world is just a little worse off.

And of course you never see any of the great results from a book...like the ones Melissa did.

The wisdom that's recorded and shared through books *should* come from the best minds on Earth, not just the people who spend time writing down their thoughts.

But right now, the only people writing books are the ones willing to endure the painful and ridiculous process that it requires.

It doesn't have to be this way. The Book In A Box Method solves this problem.

CAN YOU REALLY WRITE A BOOK THIS WAY?

Yes. This book shows you how to take the valuable knowledge out of your head and turn it into a professional book to share with the world using a simple, crystal-clear method.

The key to our process is that we remove two things from the book creation process:

1. Uncertainty on the process to write a book

2. The need to develop writing skills

This may seem crazy to you at first, just like it did to me...*how can you write a book without writing it?*

I understand the apprehension. I actually am a professional writer, and that notion seemed like nonsense to me at first too.

So, before we tackle the question of why writing doesn't have to be part of the process of creating a book, let's step back and ask ourselves a simple question:

Why do books even exist?

A book, especially a non-fiction book, exists **to take a singular, contained set of wisdom or ideas out of the head of the author and share it with readers.** Plainly put, a book is a medium of transfer for knowledge, wisdom, or ideas. That is the purpose it serves.

Then where does writing come in?

Writing is the act of recording, in the form of words and sentences, the wisdom you are sharing so someone else can consume it. The chain of causation looks like this:

Experiences and Learning Create Wisdom → Wisdom Is In Your Head → **Write Down Wisdom In Book Form** → Others Absorb Wisdom By Reading Your Book

And right there you see the problem: "Write Down Wisdom In Book Form."

The act of writing is very hard for most people. Not because people are stupid or lazy or unskilled. It's because writing is an unusual cognitive task that requires deep, specialized skill. The writing skill is a *totally different* skill from having intelligence, wisdom, experience, or knowledge to share.

Just think about it. How many really intelligent and accomplished people do you know who have all kinds of things to say, but hate writing? Quite a few, I am sure (you might even be one).

And the inverse is true, as well. How many skilled and experienced writers have you read who used so many beautiful words to effectively say nothing? Sadly, that might describe the majority of professional writers.

Another example of this: dyslexia. Some of the smartest, most accomplished people on Earth—Richard Branson, for example—can barely write an email. Richard is not stupid, nor is anyone else with dyslexia. It's just that human brains are not optimized to read or write text, and those with dyslexia are never able to efficiently develop those functions.

Writing is a specific cognitive skill that is totally distinct from thinking and wisdom. Just like the ability to do math in your head is a skill distinct from being a good mathematician (Richard Feynman often used calculators), or the ability to read sheet music is not a necessary skill to be a great musician (Jimi

Hendrix couldn't read sheet music), writing has nothing to do with anything other than the ability to write.

This begs the question: *Is the skill of writing really a necessary part of sharing knowledge and ideas?*

After all, if the ultimate goal of a book is to share your knowledge and ideas with the world, is there another way to record this wisdom without having to physically write it down yourself?

Of course there's another way to share knowledge and wisdom: talking.

After all, **talking is the natural way to communicate ideas and information between humans.** We've been talking for at least 200,000 years, but we've only been writing for about 10,000 years.

But that still leaves the work of turning the talking into a book. Is there a way for a person to talk about their wisdom and ideas, instead of writing them down, and use that talking as the basis for the book?

Yes, of course there is! People have done this through history. Here's a very short list of people whose words still move the world, yet they never wrote anything down:

- Socrates never wrote anything down, Plato recorded his words.
- Jesus Christ never wrote down a word, his disciples did.

- Buddha never wrote down any of his teachings, his disciples did that as well.
- Marco Polo told his cellmate about his travels while they were in jail, and his cellmate (who was a scribe) wrote them down.
- Winston Churchill dictated all of his books to his secretary.
- Malcolm X dictated his iconic autobiography to journalist Alex Haley.

In fact, the idea that you have to sit down and be the person who actually writes your book on paper (or a computer) is a curiosity of our recent modern time.

For thousands of years, writing was a specific job, different from thinking. People who did the writing were called "scribes," and they were not themselves the esteemed thinkers and influencers of their era (what we would now call a "thought leader"). In fact, they were considered artisans with a skill, like a lawyer or a mechanic.

Take one of the most prolific authors of the Roman age, the great Julius Caesar. He used scribes to record almost every single line in all of his letters and books.

Why did he use scribes instead of writing it himself?

For the obvious reason: his time was too valuable to be spent mastering the skill of writing words so they read properly on the page.

He spent his time thinking and doing things, not writing.

He has scribes record his thoughts as he spoke them out loud, and then he signed his name to it. His volumes of letters and correspondence are all rightly authored by him, yet he "wrote" none of the actual words down.

Okay fine, maybe a long time ago you didn't have to write a book to be the author, but what about now? Is there a way to do it systematically, in a way that anyone can use and replicate, in current times?

Yes, now there is. We think we've solved that puzzle—how to get knowledge wisdom out of a head and into a book, without you having to write it down.

There are two simple principles behind our process:

1. **Certainty of Process:** We want you to never have to figure out on your own what to do next. We tell you exactly what to do, every step of the way. By never thinking about the process, you can focus only on your ideas and wisdom.

2. **No Writing:** We don't want you to ever have to face a blank page. We will never tell you to "just write." We replace all of the writing with talking and editing.

Here's how it breaks down, and we walk you through each step in the book:

PART 1: DO YOU HAVE A BOOK IN YOU?
We teach you exactly how to examine your book idea from

the three crucial perspectives needed for success so you can figure out the exact positioning it needs.

PART 2: WRITE YOUR BOOK

With a clear book idea, we teach you how to flesh it out into an extremely detailed outline. From there, you have someone interview you to extract the content, and then translate that content into final book form. The last step is editing, which we give you a step-by-step plan for.

PART 3: PUBLISH YOUR BOOK

The final section of this book walks you through what to do once you have a completed manuscript. That includes design, formatting, and everything else you need to do to publish your book and share it with the world.

WHAT THIS MEANS TO YOU (AND THE WORLD)

This is very interesting, but what does it mean? Or more specifically, what does all of this mean to you?

Well, the most obvious thing is that **the Book In A Box method means is that you can now confidently start and finish your book.**

If you follow the process we lay out in this book, it will work, and you will end up with a good book. Our process is proven by our track record with our Book In A Box authors. We've successfully executed the exact process we are about to describe to you with hundreds of authors.

But we think this is bigger than you, bigger than one book, and much bigger than us. For us, this isn't just about writing books, per se. It's about something much bigger than that.

To put it simply, *we think books are the most important way our culture advances, and far too important to leave to writers.*

We are publishing our method because we want the wisest, most experienced, most knowledgeable people on Earth to be able to effectively and easily share their wisdom with the world. And that is what this book will show you how to do. It's about sharing knowledge and wisdom, so you can help everyone learn and advance and grow as you did.

Think about it. Where did all the valuable knowledge in your head come from? Some of it likely came from books. But most of it came from experience, or from someone teaching it to you.

This is definitely true for me, and Zach too. We have learned from a lot of smart people, people who didn't record their wisdom in a book, but instead just shared it directly with us. Their wisdom has been instrumental in helping us achieve what we've done in life, yet only a few people have access to it.

Think how many more people they could have reached with a book. Now magnify that by the tens of thousands of experienced, seasoned professionals and experts in the world, and you realize something profound: **the world is missing out on a lot of important wisdom.**

This is not a small thing. You may not realize this, but the majority of the tacit knowledge that builds civilizations, the stuff that maybe isn't sexy but is foundational knowledge, has actually been lost. Why?

Because no one wrote it down. They just passed it on by word of mouth.

Some examples:

Until recently, scientists had *no idea* how the Egyptians made the pyramids. These incredible architectural and logistical feats were accomplished over 5,000 years ago, and all that knowledge was lost until very, very recently (and even now, we aren't 100% positive about our reconstruction of their methods).

Same with the Roman aqueducts. Even to this day, we don't know how they so precisely calculated the right grade of the slope to ensure that water flowed properly, nor how they made the concrete that still holds the stones together *to this day*. More extremely valuable wisdom, lost for centuries.

In fact, part of the reason western Europe plunged into a Dark Age after the fall of Rome was because all of the tacit knowledge on how to build and maintain a civilization was locked inside the heads of the Romans—they didn't write it down. So when they died, it was lost forever. It took Europe over 1,000 years to relearn all of that wisdom and launch the Renaissance.

Let's be very specific here: we are talking about knowledge and wisdom and *not information*—we are awash in information, and Google does a great job of organizing all of it.

Wisdom is not the same thing as knowledge or information. Wisdom is information plus knowledge plus context, and only a human can do that. Wisdom is information you can actually use.

Here's a great example of the difference between information and knowledge and wisdom:

Information is knowing what a tomato is. Knowledge is knowing that tomato is a fruit. Wisdom is knowing that you'd never put a tomato into a fruit salad.

Google dominates at information, no question. If you Google "Italian restaurant in New York City," Google will list every single one.

But have you ever tried to use Google to find actual, usable wisdom? What happens when you Google "how to start a great Italian restaurant in New York City"? Good luck sorting through that mess. It's great at facts and information, but it does a terrible job turning facts and information into knowledge and wisdom you can use.

This is precisely what a well-constructed non-fiction book does: it takes information, adds contextualization, explanation, and application, and turns it into usable wisdom for people.

This is also called "tacit knowledge," and our society does a terrible job recording and sharing it (just like the ancient Romans and Egyptians did).

With all of our technology we are hardly better than the Romans or the Egyptians in this regard. Here's a great example, from one of our clients at Book In A Box:

We had a surgeon come to us with a very simple idea. He wanted to write a book that taught young surgeons how to run their surgical careers (called *The Hidden Curriculum*). Why was this necessary? Medical school teaches doctors NOTHING about the job of being a surgeon (e.g., the options available to them or how to manage their careers).

Can you believe that? A person will spend four years in school and not spend one minute learning anything about how to manage their actual career. This surgeon had decades of experience as a surgeon and had learned everything there was to know about surgical careers, and he wanted to share his wisdom with other surgeons starting off so they could benefit from his experience.

This is not a unique or isolated case. The vast majority of our author clients come to us with book ideas that make us say, "How does this not already exist?"

It doesn't, because even though our society does a great job recording and sharing *information*, it does a terrible job turning it into recorded and shared *wisdom*.

That's why we took what was only supposed to be the solution to one entrepreneur's problem and offered it to the world (both through our company and through this book):

So that the smartest, most accomplished experts and professionals can easily share their wisdom with the world.

Please, if you have important wisdom and knowledge, use the instructions in this book to record and share it with the world.

This is how the world gets better—sharing knowledge and wisdom, so that people can use it and build on it.

This is how you can make the world a better place—by sharing what valuable knowledge and wisdom you know, so everyone can use it.

Now let's get to it!

PART 1

DO YOU HAVE A BOOK IN YOU?

DO YOU HAVE A
BOOK IN YOU?

There is a clear and simple way to determine if you have a book in you. The problem is that almost nothing out there helps you understand this.

That's because virtually all of the commentary and instruction about books is geared towards professional writers—people who only make money by writing books or articles. There's a huge group of people who are almost totally unserved in terms of writing advice: smart people with good ideas who do NOT write professionally.

The place this gap in knowledge is most evident is where people are told they should start. Professional writers are told to first figure out what they want their book to be about, then what they want to say in it, and then worry about their audience.

This idea is completely wrong for anyone else (and it's not even great for professional writers, to be honest).

If you are writing a book, the best place to start is not a deep dive into what's in the book, but rather, **why you are writing the book**. Then you can understand where the book fits into the market, if there is an audience for it, and only then do you worry about what is actually in it.

In essence, in order to know if you have a book in you, you must answer the questions:

1. *Why are you writing this book?*

2. *Who will care about this book?*

3. *Why will they care?*

THIS IS CALLED "POSITIONING"

For one hundred years in old media traditional publishing, this process was called "positioning," and every agent had this discussion with editors about a book before they sold it.

Strictly speaking, in traditional publishing circles the positioning discussion only revolved around how the book fit into traditional sales categories. That's where the term comes from. It's literally a discussion of what *position* in the bookstore shelves the book is supposed to fit in, because in the 20th century, the market for books was essentially synonymous with the needs of bookstores.

This is obviously no longer the case. The majority of books are now sold digitally, and the majority of physical books are sold in non-book retail stores like Costco and Walmart.

But this does not mean positioning is no longer important. *Positioning is the most crucial part of writing your book, and that's why we start there.*

But we don't start at the old starting place. This is because something else has changed in publishing: why books are even written to begin with.

When all book publishing was done by traditional publishing companies, then the only positioning they cared about was what a reader would BUY. In essence, publishers only cared about books that had the potential to sell a lot of copies, because that's how they made money.

But that's not true anymore. Now, most books are published outside of the old traditional models, and now, most non-fiction books are not monetized directly. In fact, quite the opposite; *most non-fiction authors make all of their money from books indirectly.*

Directly making money from books is by selling copies, of course. Indirectly making money from books means you are using a book as a marketing tool to get you something else that makes you money. For example, a book can be used to get you:

- Paid speaking gigs
- Consulting jobs

* Coaching clients
* Leads for your business

This fundamentally changes the way books are conceived and positioned (more on this later).

At Book In A Box, we've adapted the old traditional positioning process so that instead of serving the needs of the publishing company, it serves the needs of you (the author).

We do this by starting with the author in mind, then focus on the reader, and only then worry about the content. This is a specific process that we developed at Book In A Box after taking hundreds of authors through the book creation process. It works extremely well if you use it properly.

What follows are the exact steps and questions we use with real authors to help them refine and crystallize their ideas into books that will get them results. Part 1 of this book will enable you to crystalize your book by helping you answer these three questions:

1. *What result must the book produce to make it a success for you?*

2. *What audience must you reach for the book to achieve these results?*

3. *What do you have to say that is interesting and valuable to that audience?*

WHAT RESULT MUST THIS BOOK PRODUCE TO BE A SUCCESS?

At Book In A Box, the first conversation we have with an author is about the result they want from their book.

Knowing the specific result you want to achieve allows you to focus only on those efforts that will get you that result.

Thus, your book topic is wholly dependent on the result you want it to create for you.

For example, if your goal is to keynote speeches and major conferences, then the requirements for your book and are very different than if your goal is to write a book that establishes your credibility and authority in a specific field so you can build a consulting business.

Ultimately, we want the book to actually be effective for our author (you). By knowing specifically what you want to accomplish, you won't get bogged down by trying to be everything to everyone and instead you can focus on a specific plan of action that will get you what you want.

This is not a small point, and in fact, this is possibly the most crucial part of this book:

You MUST be honest with yourself about what results are important to you, or your book will fail—commercially, personally, or both.

Part of the problem here is that some results are things people feel uncomfortable admitting to. It might feel embarrassing or weird to say you're writing a book to be recognized for your contributions to a field. But you'll never get that if you don't acknowledge it first.

A key point to understand (before you get discouraged) is that there is almost no such thing as a wrong or bad goal. There is only a wrong or bad book for certain specific goals.

For example, if you wrote a book about the history of pieced quilting in colonial America, your chances of turning that into a major bestseller are almost zero. That subject is just not interesting to very many people. Either your goal or your topic needs to change, or your book won't be a success for you.

If, instead, your goal is to be perceived as an authority on the history of quilting, and give speeches about it to quilting groups, then your goal is absolutely reachable.

And if you *must* write a bestseller, for whatever reason, then you need to reexamine your choice of topic and pick something that has more commercial appeal than quilting.

COMMON RESULTS AUTHORS CAN GET FROM BOOKS

There are many things a book can get you. You can even go after several different results at one time, and they can overlap, so don't assume there is some prescribed number as you begin to evaluate your options.

This list is just to give you an idea of the most common ones we hear from authors.

1. Generate authority and visibility in your field

This is one of the best reasons to write a book. If you know something that is unique, valuable, or rarely understood by people, then sharing it with the world is not only very beneficial to the public, it also greatly raises your status, and enables people to recognize you for the authority that you are.

Furthermore, using a book to help influence what people think is one of the most effective ways to contribute to the world of ideas and can lead to a lot of other opportunities for the author. That's why it is one of the more common goals we see as book publishers.

Books hold a unique position in our culture and function as a strong signal that the author knows what they are talking about on a subject. Not only that, but if your book is solid and gets recommended by other influencers in your field, it can establish you as an influencer and help serve other goals you may have.

Example: Our very first client at Book In A Box, Melissa Gonzalez, was a trailblazer and authority in her field of pop-up retail. To give you some context, Melissa is one of the world's foremost experts on pop-up retail. She helps companies like Marc Jacobs and Chanel set up their pop-up shops, and she's great at it.

The problem was that very few people knew who she was. By writing a book that taught other people what she knew in that field, she established herself as an authority.

And even better, because her book was the first one in her niche, it got her in front of the influencers in the retail space—like people in the press and conference organizers and major retail decision makers—and her reputation skyrocketed.

The book has only been out for about 18 months, and it's only sold about 2000 copies—but it's already led to Melissa giving keynote speeches at conferences in New York, Texas, and Amsterdam, and being featured hundreds of times in the press in outlets like Forbes, Bloomberg, and CNBC.

She even got a radio show called Retail with Melissa on ABC, and a monthly column retail with The New York Daily News.

Because the book was so deeply focused on the interests of decision makers in her space, it was easy for her to market it.

She focused ONLY on the people who care about retail, and got a lot of attention from them.

This influence turned into results for her. Inbound inquiries for her firm doubled. And not only did she increase the quantity of leads, but also the quality.

About two months after the book came out, Melissa went into the office to find a voicemail from the CEO of a major mall group. He'd read her book and realized that the pop-up trend was not just a fad, and he was interested in implementing pop-ups in his malls across the country, to stay ahead of the curve.

Melissa ended up signing a seven-figure consulting deal with the mall group to help make that happen. All from a book that taught the world what she knew.

Things to Consider If This Is Your Goal: It makes sense to understand precisely why you care about influencing what people think about your subject. What are you going to do with that influence? How do you want to use it? Where do you want it to lead? The answers to these questions impact the content of your book at every level (we cover this more in the audience section, below).

2. Generate leads for a business or service

A book is a great way to market a business or a service, especially in smaller niches. Writing a basic book about a subject draws a ton of attention to your company from the very people you most want to reach: those who are looking for information about what you do.

Example: Josh Turner had a very successful consultancy when he approached us to do a book, *Connect*. He wanted to create a book that explained what he did and how he did it, which would accomplish two goals:

1. It would help people who *couldn't* afford him to achieve as much as they could on their own.

2. It would show potential clients who *could* afford him exactly what he did and how complicated it was, and persuade them to hire him.

It worked. Since Josh's book came out (and hit the *Wall Street Journal* Bestseller List), his consultancy has grown 300%.

Things to Consider If This Is Your Goal: This type of book cannot just be a sales document or a promotional brochure for your company. It *must* provide real value to customers and, more importantly, be marketed in a way that makes that value clear.

For many people, this means giving away information you would normally charge for, so prepare yourself for that if this is one of your goals. But the point is not to give everything away, the point is to only pull in the customers and clients who are right for you and your service.

3. Get speaking engagements

This is often tied to being a thought leader, but not always. The point is, most organizations and conferences that book speakers like to have some external social proof that the speaker they are considering is qualified to talk about the subject being covered.

We informally call it the "Book As Business Card" goal, and a book can be very effective in opening up all sorts of speaking opportunities for you as the author.

Example: There are so many examples it's hard to point to just one, simply because even our authors who don't write a book for this reason get asked to do speeches.

A great example is Cameron Herold, the famous CEO coach. He had no shortage of speaking events, but he wanted to speaking about different topics, to a different audience. So we did not one, but three, books with him over the course of a year, and now he has doubled both his speaking fee and his booked speeches, while opening up his ability to talk to different types of groups.

4. Share an important idea or piece of wisdom that helps people
This is similar to being a thought leader or influencer but more focused on the spreading of important ideas or wisdom and less about your specific personal goals.

It's the difference between being a political theorist (who's a thought leader) and drawing attention to how abortion laws have impacted low-income women in Appalachia, for example (that's a specific cause).

Be careful of having a vague goal of just "helping people." If you can't specifically talk about exactly how your book will help people, then this is just a wish and not an actual goal.

Example: Dr. David Kashmer wanted to give back to the medical community and to doctors. There were many ways he could probably do that, but the one that stood out was teaching surgeons the career options available to them, and how to manage them. Shockingly, this is NOT taught in medical school, and is extremely valuable. In fact, it can be the difference between surgeons staying in the profession or leaving.

His book, *The Hidden Curriculum: What They Don't Teach You at Medical School*, is already considered a classic among young surgeons. And as an added bonus, Dr. Kashmer is now speaking widely and consulting on this issue with surgeons.

5. Launch or advance a career

For many professions, a book is necessary for serious advancement. This is a great book goal, and we've seen many clients put their knowledge and wisdom into books that then directly helped them climb a professional ladder.

In some cases, the goal of the book vis-à-vis the author's career is to help them move from one professional arena into a different, but related, one that is still connected to the author's field of expertise; an area, that is, where they would like to grow.

Example: We worked with an author, Simon Dudley, who was a prominent figure in the teleconferencing industry. He was well known as an expert in his field. The problem was that he didn't believe in his field. He was starting to put the pieces together about a bigger global trend about innovation, and he realized that the teleconferencing industry was in trouble.

Simon's book, *The End of Certainty*, breaks down his philosophy on how technology evolves. The goal of the book was to get him out of his role as an evangelist for the telecom industry, and develop his thought leadership in this new direction, so that he could launch a speaking and consulting career helping companies facing these "excession events" (as he calls them) work through the transition.

Things to Consider If This Is Your Goal: We don't recommend that authors put a book out with just anything in it. It can be tempting to throw something together and call it a book, but this tactic can backfire. Make sure you have something substantive to say first, and be very clear about what career result you want your book to help you achieve.

MISTAKES AUTHORS OFTEN MAKE WHEN FRAMING RESULTS

We did say earlier that there are no "bad reasons" for writing a book. That is true, sort of. There are definitely reasons that people have that are not optimal, and will end up hurting the book. Here are the main four results that tend to lead to bad decisions:

Bad Reason #1: "I want to sell millions of books and make a lot of money."

I hate to be the one to crush your dreams, but the odds that it will sell even 100,000 copies are so vanishingly small they are essentially zero.

Last year, there were about 300,000 books published[1]—just in America. According to BookScan,[2] only about 200 books per year reach a 100,000 copies sold.[3] That means you have, statistically, about a 0.007% chance of selling one-tenth of a million, much less a million.

The number that reach 1 million sold is even fewer, probably close to 10. And virtually no book does more than that. In fact, the list of books that have sold 10 million copies in HISTORY is so small there is a Wikipedia page about them.[4]

The return on time invested for authors is horrendous when you measure it in terms of the expected value of book sales. It's basically the same thing as saying that your retirement strategy is to "play the lottery." Yeah, someone has to win the lottery, but your lifetime ROI on that investment strategy is probably going to be negative. In fact, your odds of winning most lotteries[5] are better than selling a million books.

You are not selling millions of copies and getting rich on book sales, and if you write a book for that reason, you'll be disappointed. That's the bad news.

1   https://en.wikipedia.org/wiki/Books_published_per_country_per_year

2   https://en.wikipedia.org/wiki/Nielsen_BookScan

3   https://www.quora.com/Books/How-many-people-each-year-write-a-book-that-gets-100-000-copies-sold

4   https://en.wikipedia.org/wiki/List_of_best-selling_books

5   https://en.wikipedia.org/wiki/Lottery_mathematics

What's the Better Version of This Goal?

The good news is that a book CAN make you money, if you look at it from a totally different perspective. Instead of trying to get rich by *selling* millions of copies, if you look at a book as a way to generate attention for your other endeavors, then the path to profit can become wide and smooth.

For example, if you have some skill or knowledge that is very valuable to people, the best way to build a consultancy and sell that knowledge is by writing a book that shows what you know (like Melissa and Josh). This establishes you as an authority and gives you credibility to sell your services (and charge a premium), as well as giving you a consistent pipeline of people looking for the exact type of skill and experience you offer.

This is using a book to make money, but doing it an indirect way. It's using the book as a platform to promote something else, especially something expensive and profitable (and usually hard to promote, like consulting skills).

You can think of the book as a business card, or general marketing material. The fact is, books not only possess a credibility that very few marketing materials do, they are a great way to differentiate yourself in crowded fields, and a great way to find people who have the exact problems that you can solve, and connect with them.

How does that happen? Well, one way: Amazon is the third largest search engine in the world, and the *largest search engine for professionals.*

Think about it—how many times have you had a problem, and tried to solve it by finding a book about it?

Well, what if you were the person who WROTE the book on how to solve that problem? Then you're going to get all those people coming to you.

This doesn't work for everyone, but does work really well for companies, entrepreneurs, coaches, consultants, and even certain types of executives.

Bad Reason #2: "I want to be a famous, bestselling author."
Everyone wants to be famous, and some people think a book will do that. I've already explained why rich won't happen (except indirectly), and the worse news is that a book is even less likely to make you famous than rich.

Yes, yes, there are famous authors. But far fewer than you think.

In fact, there are only about 15 or 20 (living) people who are famous ONLY for writing (and nothing else). Malcolm Gladwell is one. J.K. Rowling is another. You can probably name five more. But probably not 10 more, and definitely not 20 more. Start naming famous writers, and you'll realize quickly that 80% or more of your list are dead (Hemingway, Twain, Lee, Tolkien, etc.).

The fact is, writers are just not celebrities in America anymore. In fact, it goes the other way around in most cases; people get famous for something else first, THEN they write a book that becomes a bestseller. Being famous is usually *why their book sells*; they don't get famous from their book.

Here's the worst part of getting fame from books: hitting a bestseller list does NOT mean you will become famous.

Just like having the line "These pretzels are making me thirsty" in a small indie movie isn't putting you on the cover of *People*, having a book that spends a week or two on *The New York Times* bestseller list does not mean you're famous. It barely gets you any attention at all.

Here's a fun game that shows this: What're your three favorite books? Were any of those books bestsellers?

When I ask this of people, there's usually a stunned silence, and then the inevitable answer, "Wow. Yeah...I have no idea."

Because being a bestseller has virtually no bearing on the fame or impact of a book! There are thousands of books that hit the bestseller list for a week and no one reads or hears about them again, and yet many of the most impactful books in the world have *never been* bestsellers.

It's true; not only do books almost never make you famous, *even having a bestselling book won't make you famous!*

What's the Better Version of This Goal?

Ask yourself: why do you care if your book is a bestseller?

If it's just for the status—just so you can brag to people at parties—then you need to re-examine your goal. You're only doing this for ego reasons, and nothing else, and quite frankly, there are much easier, cheaper ways to get an ego boost than spending a year writing a book and then a ton of time and money promoting it.

But, if all you want is the recognition and validation that comes from making a contribution to the world, that is TOTALLY doable, and a book is a great way to both give to the world AND get recognized for that giving.

The problem comes with the thinking that a bestseller is the measure of your book's contribution to the world.

If you reframe your goal from, "I want to be a famous bestselling author," to something that is closer to what you actually want, like, "I want my book to make an impact on lives and get some recognition for that," then it does two things:

1. It makes the goal very achievable.

2. It actually helps you to write a better book.

How does it make the book better? Because if your goal is just to help people and be recognized for that, you can almost always teach something to at least a few thousand people that greatly impacts their lives.

Doing that might not sell enough copies to be a bestseller, but it *will* help those people, and they will thank you and recognize you for it.

And isn't that the point?

Bad Reason #3: "I want to live the writer's life."

I think this is summed up perfectly by Hugh Macleod, the awesome cartoonist and author:

"A successful book agent I know tells me that at least half the people he meets who are writing their first book, are doing so not because they have anything particularly interesting to say, but because the idea of 'the writer's life' appeals to them. Tweed jackets, smoking a pipe, sitting out in the gazebo and getting sloshed on Mint Juleps, pensively typing away at an old black Remington. Bantering wittily at all the right parties. Or whatever. Anybody who wants to write books for this reason deserves to suffer. And happily, many of them do."

Doesn't this seem like so many other things? We all say we want to be rich, lose weight, start a business, etc.

But it's the idea of being rich or skinny or an entrepreneur that's more appealing than actually doing it. The idea sounds glamorous, and we want glamour.

But we don't get glamour by "living the writer's life," or by wearing the best gym clothes, or playing the "startup game."

Glamour is the RESULT of hard work and doing something that other people find valuable. Notice what's missing when people say that? Actual writing.

What's the Better Version of This Goal?

This is about identity. Who do you want to be? "Living the

writer's life" is fine, if that's who you are.

But you probably aren't. Instead, don't go looking for an identity. Either embrace the identity you have, or work REALLY hard to create the identity you want.

This is a long way of saying there is no way to have the privileges and glamour and status of an identity, without doing the work necessary to get that identity.

And with a book, this doesn't mean "living a writer's life." It means authoring a book that other people actually want to read.

Bad Reason #4: "I don't care what anyone thinks, I'm just writing this for myself."
This type of "book" has a name already: a diary.

If this is your goal—yes, many people have said this to me, and yes, it's a perfectly valid goal—then consider that all you need to do is write it, but not release it.

I'm serious. I have several friends who write just for themselves, and they don't do anything with the writing at all. This is perfectly fine. But there's no reason to publish it. Or even talk about it. If it's just for you, let it just be for you. You don't need to do anything else.

The point is, this statement is usually a lie authors tell themselves to protect against failure. Many people who say this, then go on to not only publish their writing that was "just for them" but also make huge efforts to promote it.

Why, if it's just for them?

What's the Better Version of This Goal?

There is none. Just go write it for the reasons you want, and leave it in a drawer, and you're good.

Or, recognize that you DO want recognition for you book, and then focus on writing a book that will be appealing and helpful to other people.

HOW TO FIGURE OUT THE RESULT YOU WANT

We're sure some of those results resonated with you, but possibly you're not clear on exactly what you're hoping to accomplish. This next section is designed to do precisely that: help you figure out the specific results you want your book to achieve.

Questions To Ask Yourself:

Why do I want to write a book?

It is easy to fool yourself here, so be careful. The first question about goals will often be met with some bullshit, socially acceptable answer. Don't accept that from yourself. The more honest you are with yourself, the better you will be able to create a book.

What specific result(s) must I have to make this book a success for me?

This question forces you to nail down a specific, definable result you want from the book. Often you'll have many different goals, and some either take a while to come out, or are even hidden from your conscious thought. The more you know about the specific results you are looking for—business leads, client consulting gigs, attention—the more you can guide the book to get that result.

THE DOUBLE CHECK QUESTION: CREATE
A WORST-CASE SCENARIO

A good way to really nail yourself to a specific result is to create a scenario that meets your stated goals but fails in all other regards.

So for example, if you say your goal is to just have a book that you can put on your résumé and maybe sell at your current speaking gigs, then a question you need to ask yourself is something like this:

"So if the book comes out, sells no copies, and gets no attention, but it looks very professional and I can sell it at speaking gigs and put it on my résumé, would I be happy with that result?"

If you can honestly say yes, great, you're done here.

If you hem and haw and equivocate, then you need to drill deeper and make sure you nail down precisely what other goals must be included in this scenario for you to be satisfied with the result.

WHO IS THE AUDIENCE FOR YOUR BOOK?

Now that you have a good idea as to what results you want from your book, you can start thinking about how to achieve those results.

In order to get those results—no matter what they are—the book must find some sort of audience. It can be huge and broad, or it can be small and focused, but it must exist.

HOW TO FIGURE OUT YOUR AUDIENCE

Remember that the audience you need to reach is directly tied to the results you picked, and you can reverse engineer precisely who your audience is by understanding who literally needs to know about your book to make your results happen. This process is not much more complicated than asking yourself a very basic question:

"Who has to know about my book in order for it to get the results I want?"

For example, if you want to speak at a major oil and gas conference, then your audience is composed of the people who book the speakers for that specific conference (and maybe the attendees).

If you want clients for your CTO coaching business, then chief technology officers (and the people who know them) are your audience.

If you want your book to establish you as a thought leader, then your audience is the people who care about the issues relevant to your space or who are influencers in your space.

If you want to drive business to your consulting firm, then your audience is potential clients.

If you want to develop a speaking career, then your audience is composed of the people who book the events where you want to speak.

YOU MUST BE SPECIFIC

You can absolutely have multiple audiences that the book will appeal to, but generally speaking, the more audiences you try to reach, the worse your book will be.

A focused book that is very appealing to a small audience is usually much more valuable than a broad subject book that is only marginally appealing to a lot of audiences. This is because broad subjects, like general life advice, tend to not only be well-covered already, but also tend to not be very actionable for people.

Most people read non-fiction because they expect it to provide a positive impact or ROI in their lives. It is clear who the audience for a book about how to set up a pop-up retail experience is. Even though it's a small audience, the audience is very interested in it.

Compare this to a book about a broad, general topic, like "how to be happy." You might think everyone cares about being happy, and that is true to some extent, but unless you are really knowledgeable and already an expert about this subject AND you have an angle that has never been explored, it will be very hard to convince people that your book about happiness—as opposed to the 70 already out there by experts—is the one to read.

Also, please do not think that "everyone" is your audience. That is never an answer to this question; no book idea appeals to everyone. You must be specific.

The more specific you are, the better. "Young women" is not specific. "Single women aged 18-30 who work in the fashion industry and are looking for a husband" is specific.

BEWARE: THIS MIGHT CHANGE EVERYTHING

The answer to this question is wholly dependent on the results you want. If you don't like the audience you realized you must reach, then you have to pick a different book result.

Be prepared for this to lead to a change to the answer about your goals. Many authors who go through this exercise realize that they don't actually have the knowledge to write a book that will achieve their first goal, but instead do have the knowledge to write a book that will achieve another goal they want, or even some other goal they had not originally considered.

Always keep this in mind as you consider who your audience is and how you can reach them:

The absolute best outcome is when the author's goals and the reader's goals can align. That makes for great books.

Example: We had an author who had lived an incredibly interesting life and had some amazing stories. He wanted a book of his life stories, but he also wanted the book to resonate with people and change lives. He wanted people to enjoy and recommend the book to others because of the impact it had on them.

We pressed him to understand why anyone would care about his stories. Other than being somewhat interesting, what is in it for them? Since they don't know him or care about him, what about his stories matters to them? What can they learn? How can his stories make their lives better?

After much consideration, he realized that he had quite a bit to teach people about how to integrate meaning into their lives using altruistic charity work. He had done things that few people have done, but many want to do (overseas charity work building orphanages, for example), and laid out a precise, specific set of instructions about how a normal person could do these things.

This turned the book from a semi-interesting series of stories about him into an engaging book about how someone can help other people. It taught a lesson that people wanted to hear and did it the best way possible—by using personal examples from his interesting stories. This is the best of both worlds.

CHAPTER 4

WHAT DO YOU HAVE TO SAY THAT'S INTERESTING AND VALUABLE TO YOUR AUDIENCE?

It is crucial that you save the description of precisely what is in the book for *after* the discussions of goals and audience, because if you don't, the process of organizing and outlining the book becomes exponentially harder.

Why is this?

Because without an idea of what result you want and who your target audience is, the content of the book has no anchor in any objective reality and can float into any number of places.

Once you know your desired results and who the audience for the book is, you can determine precisely what your book has to be in order to reach your audience and thus get to your results.

What you know that your audience will find interesting and take value from determines the content of the book.

HOW TO FIGURE OUT WHAT'S INTERESTING AND VALUABLE TO YOUR AUDIENCE

For many authors, this is the first time they've thought about their book from *the perspective of the audience*. They've only dreamed about the reaction an audience will have to their book and not spent any time thinking about **why** the audience will react that way.

Think about yourself as you decide to buy a book. Do you ever think about the author's concerns?

Of course you don't. You think about **why buying this book might help you.**

Well, that's precisely what your audience is going to do when they see your book on a shelf or Amazon or their friend's Facebook page. So you had better be able to answer that question:

Why does your book matter to them?

These are the questions we use to help authors answer this question:

What is the essential point(s) you are making for your audience? What are the main points you want the audience to take away from your book?

This should get all the main points out and into a list. From this list, you will later organize and create the book outline. At the end of this question, ideally you will have the major points and chapters identified and be able to then fill in all the details under each heading in the outline.

What, specifically, will your audience get by reading your book? How does your book help your audience achieve their goals?

Push yourself to focus on specific statements of value that the book will deliver to your specific audience, not broad, oblique wishes. The answer to your questions should be something clear and definable, not ambiguous.

You have to remember that your book is competing with an infinite amount of other media, much of it immediately consumable for free. To overcome that, you must appeal to the self-interest of your potential reader, and identifying what about your book will interest them. Putting yourself in their shoes is how you do that.

What is the story your audience told themselves (about the world, about their situations, about their perceptions) before they started your book? How does your book fit into those stories, and what part does it play?

This is another way to approach the question to really get inside the head of your reader / audience and understand them, so you can craft your book to best reach them. This question forces you to look at them and their lives as a whole, and understand where your book fits into their world view, so you can best fit into it.

Remember: You don't have to know exactly what your book is about at this point to answer this question. You just have to know what that audience wants from their lives, and whether or not you have some knowledge or wisdom you can share to help them get it.

What does this mean your book should be about?

This should be a very short statement that summarizes the book subject at its core. This should be no longer than a sentence or two. Imagine what a reader would tell their friend if they were asked, "That book you're reading, what's it about?"

What background information does the reader need to have to understand your points above? How do you plan to explain all the background information that the reader needs?

This is NOT intended to be a brain dump, but simply a listing of some basic things you need to make sure you don't assume your audience knows.

THE DOUBLE CHECK QUESTION: HOW WILL PEOPLE DESCRIBE THIS BOOK TO THEIR FRIENDS?

This is an important exercise that helps with positioning. We use this when an author will insist on a certain angle or idea that we know will not work. Instead of arguing with them, the best way to get them to understand is to ask them this question:

"Picture your ideal reader. How do you envision that person describing your book to their friends at a party?"

This is the *real* core answer, not the answer the author wants people to say. Amazon founder and CEO Jeff Bezos says that branding (which is almost the same thing as positioning) is "what people say about you when you aren't there." This is the same idea: what will people *really* say about this book, not what you *hope* they say.

We've found that this question helps the author see the content in the book from the reader's perspective, and not just their own, and thus helps us convince the author to position the book in a way that serves the interests of the reader.

We have also used this question successfully to talk authors out of bad book titles and positioning, and into good ones. The key here is to understand two things:

1. The only effective book marketing is word of mouth.

2. People share books for limited reasons.

Generally speaking, people actively share books (or anything) if:

1. The book makes them look smart, successful, or high status, and / or

2. They took a lot of value from the book, and / or

3. In some way they associate the book with an identity they desire, and want to broadcast it to the world.

For example, if the book has a whole new take on an old industry, sharing it with their friends will make them look smart, educated, and well-read.

If the book helped them lose 50 pounds, they'll talk about it because people will praise them for losing all that weight, and sharing this information will raise their status among their friends.

If the book is about how to integrate the Bible into their marriage (and they are Christian), they'll talk about it because it tells the world (and their Christian friends) precisely how Christian they really are (which reinforces their Christian identity).

On the other hand, people actively do **not** share things that:

1. Make them feel stupid, and / or

2. Make them look low status to their friends, and / or

3. Are hard to explain.

For example, if the book title is hard to pronounce, people won't say it out loud at a party because they will feel stupid for not knowing how to pronounce it.

If the book is something that is looked down on by their friends—for example, if they are conspicuously Christian and the book is on how to integrate BDSM into a marriage—they probably won't admit to reading it, even if they really enjoy it.

And even if the book is great, but the reader struggles to easily explain what it's about, they are less likely to recommend it or talk about it.

CAUTION: ARE YOU TRYING TO PUT EVERYTHING YOU KNOW INTO ONE BOOK?

Many authors will try to pack everything they know into one book.

This doesn't work.

The fact is, they do this because they think they don't have enough information for one book.

The reality is, if you are an accomplished professional with deep experience in your field, you probably have multiple books in you. But that being said, the worst thing you can do is cram everything into one book. It results in a bloated, meandering mess that is hard to describe to people and has no natural audience.

The key here is to focus on your goals and how to best achieve them. If you have done that, and nailed down a specific audience, then the ideal book idea to reach that audience should emerge.

Remember: You can always write another book. You don't have to put it all into one book.

CONCLUSION

Do NOT proceed to the next steps until you have the answers to these three questions:

1. What result must the book produce to make it a success for you?

Answer: _____

2. What audience must you reach for the book to achieve this result?

Answer: _____

3. What do you have to say that is interesting and valuable to that audience?

Answer: _____

WRITE YOUR BOOK

CREATE YOUR
BOOK OUTLINE

Now you know what results you want, what audience you must reach, and what your book needs to be about in order to reach that audience. The next stage in the process is organizing your book idea into an outline.

Ironically, the more effort you put into the outline, the less the reader is going to notice or be conscious of the organization, which is what you want.

First, we're going to show you a generic outline template. Then we'll explain each section and what needs to go in it so you can apply it to your own book. Finally, we'll show you an example of an outline that is filled out.

GENERIC OUTLINE TEMPLATE

[INSERT WORKING TITLE]: *[INSERT SUBTITLE]* by [INSERT AUTHOR NAME]

The Promise / Value Proposition / Quick Summary:
• [INSERT BOOK DESCRIPTION AND PROMISE]

Author Goal(s):
• [INSERT PRIMARY AUTHOR GOAL]
• [INSERT SECONDARY AUTHOR GOAL]
• [INSERT TERTIARY AUTHOR GOAL]

Anticipated Audience(s) (And Their Benefit from Reading the Book):
• [INSERT PRIMARY AUDIENCE] + [INSERT BENEFIT]
• [INSERT SECONDARY AUDIENCE] + [INSERT BENEFIT]
• [INSERT TERTIARY AUDIENCE] + [INSERT BENEFIT]

Table of Contents
Introduction

PART 1: [INSERT WORKING TITLE]
Chapter 1: [Insert Working Chapter Title]
Chapter 2: [Insert Working Chapter Title]

PART 2: [INSERT WORKING TITLE]
Chapter 3: [Insert Working Chapter Title]
Chapter 4: [Insert Working Chapter Title]

PART 3: [INSERT WORKING TITLE]
Chapter 5: [Insert Working Chapter Title]
Chapter 6: [Insert Working Chapter Title]
Chapter 7: [Insert Working Chapter Title]

Conclusion

Book Outline
Introduction: *[INSERT TITLE]*

1. What Is the Hook?
2. What Is the Pain of Not Reading the Book?
3. What Is the Pleasure of Reading the Book?
4. What Will the Reader Learn?

Part 1: [INSERT TITLE]

[INSERT DESCRIPTION—Brief summary of the first section of the book for the interviewer to read to grasp the general flow of ideas]

Chapter 1: *[INSERT TITLE]*—[INSERT DESCRIPTION]

[INSERT SUBPOINT 1]
- [INSERT QUESTION / STORY 1]
  → [Optional: INSERT SUPPORT]
- [INSERT QUESTION / STORY 2]
  → [Optional: INSERT SUPPORT]

[INSERT SUBPOINT 2]
- [INSERT QUESTION / STORY 1]
  → [Optional: INSERT SUPPORT]
- [INSERT QUESTION / STORY 2]
  → [Optional: INSERT SUPPORT]

[EVERYTHING THE SAME AS ABOVE, REPEATED FOR PARTS 2 AND 3]

Conclusion

1. Reworded Thesis
   b. Optional—Alternate: Story that summarizes book, the "summary hook")
2. Summary of All the Main Points
3. Where To Learn More / Call To Action Page

Here we explain each section of the outline, the purpose it serves, and how best to set it up.

The Promise / Value Proposition / Quick Summary

This is why someone in your audience would want to read this book. It's what they would expect to get out of it; essentially, this the answer to the third question (what do you have to say that is interesting and valuable to your audience).

Author Goal(s)

These are your results you want for the book.

Anticipated Audience(s) (And Their Benefit from Reading the Book)

This is the specific audience you want to reach.

Table of Contents

Having a table of contents in the outline helps you organize your thoughts and see the progression of the ideas easily.

Introduction

Most authors think the purpose of the introduction is to lay out and explain everything the author will talk about in the book. That is boring and wrong.

The *actual* purpose of a good introduction is to engage the reader and make them want to read the book. It should be framed more as an interesting sales pitch rather than an informational piece (though it does serve both purposes).

To achieve this goal, you need to generally do three things in the introduction:

1. Hook the Reader (what's interesting about the book?)

2. Show Them Pain and Pleasure (explain orientation material)

3. Tell Them What They'll Learn (make a thesis statement)

This is a simple formula, and virtually all the best books you've ever read have an introduction that follows this exact process.

STRUCTURE THE PARTS

Dividing your book into parts is relatively simple. The question you need to ask yourself is this: *Are there major divisions of my story where I need to signal that this is a different thing entirely?*

This is not the same thing as chapters. For example, if you want to write a book teaching someone exactly how to become a firefighter, then the major parts could be deciding if the job is right for you, the written exam, and the physical exam. Just three parts. But each part would have two to four chapters under it. For example, the written exam part of the book would have a chapter on what's on the exam, preparing for the exam, and taking the exam.

And not all books need divided parts. You can simply list chapters if you feel that's right. Dividing your book into parts makes sense if you need to further organize information for the reader.

STRUCTURE THE CHAPTERS AND SUBPOINTS

This is where the outline starts to really take form. Chapters are the way you divide your information and wisdom into digestible chunks for people and ensure that it flows smoothly.

Each chapter needs to be broken down into subpoints, questions / stories, and (optional) support. This makes it simple for you to talk through your ideas in the interview part, and provide the content for your book.

This is VERY different from most outlines. For most outlines, nothing about questions is mentioned. The reason we tell you to structure your main points below the chapters as questions is because this is how you avoid writing, and instead will create the rough draft of your book through talking. You basically interview yourself and answer the questions.

Here is the generic layout of a chapter. We will explain each part in detail below.

Chapter 1: [Insert Title]

[INSERT SUBPOINT 1]

- [INSERT QUESTION / STORY 1]
   → [Optional: INSERT SUPPORT]
- [INSERT QUESTION / STORY 2]
   → [Optional: INSERT SUPPORT]

A chapter is simply a singular, distinct point you are making. It should include all the discussion and explanation you need for that point, divided into subpoints and stories you want to make/tell about that specific point.

Here's a sample structure from a chapter we did in a book about being a surgeon (called *The Hidden Curriculum*). Locum Tenens, which translates from Latin as "to hold a place" and in surgical terms means a physician who is temporarily filling in for another physician, is the chapter title and what the chapter is about, and everything beneath that is a subpoint:

Chapter 3: Locum Tenens

- *What is it?*
- *Who is it good and bad for?*
- *How to get jobs?*
  - → *Go through a matching company (and, preferably, a company like the author's that also helps with all the rest of the details)*
  - → *Feel free to try them all! Because you're a "freelancer" you can serve multiple companies at the same time*
- *How do I succeed at locums?*
  - → *Get armed with all the right information before!*
  - → *Where to eat, people's phone numbers, how the practice runs, what it's like there, etc.*
- *How to maintain quality?*
  - → *Explain why it's usually not a functional system you're working at, or they wouldn't need you*
  - → *How can a surgeon maintain his reputation?*

→ *How can a surgeon maintain his quality of your service in a less than functional system?*

- *How much do locums surgeons make, compared to traditional ones?*
    - → *There's no data on the locums industry as a whole, but in general, locums surgeons will make more per hour, and they should be able to fill their schedules*
    - → *The problem is the taxation, so it's important to set up a corporate entity in order to make sure your take-home income is higher*
    - → *There's just a wider variance*

What Is a Subpoint?

Quite simply, the subpoints are the pieces of explanation and support for the point you are making.

How to create subpoints: There are two standard ways we create the subpoints:

1. **Obvious subpoints of the chapter:** If the purpose of the chapter is to cover some set of separate but related ideas, like Ten Ways Doing Handstands Improves Your Health, then the subpoints are those ten reasons. Oftentimes, it's not quite this obvious, but when the purpose of a chapter is to make a point, the subpoints are usually the support for that point.

2. **The sentences that make up the logical flow of the argument:** This one is a little trickier, but it works really well. If the purpose of the chapter is to make a more subtle argument, the easiest way to arrive at the subpoints is to

write up a short paragraph that explains that argument. By breaking up that paragraph into its constituent sentences, you're left with the ideas that must be explained and proved in order to make that argument—which are the subpoints.

What Is A Question / Story Prompt?

Simply put, the questions and story prompts are what you put in to prompt the interviewer to ask you the right questions, to make sure you can talk about your topic.

How to Create Questions / Stories: Once the subpoints are filled in, choosing the right questions and stories is much simpler. Ask yourself:

What questions need to be asked and answered in order to prove the point that the subpoint is making?

Often, these are focused on "Why is this true?" and "Why is this important?" It'll also include any questions necessary to pull the relevant details.

Stories are much simpler. We use the syntax "Story: [INSERT PROMPT]" to indicate the appropriate place for a story. This is a prompt for you to tell a story that is relevant to that section.

Note: You should make sure the stories are specific and highly relevant. You are not looking for a generic story in these points; rather, this should be a story that fits precisely here and shows something you are trying to display.

If you want to find a story to fit a part, don't talk about general things. Remember, the point is to tell stories that teach or show the reader something. To do this, you really need to talk about specific times something happened. For example:

What's the best time you ever [insert topic]?

What's the worst example of [insert topic]?

What's the first time you did [insert topic], and what happened?

What's the most scared / happy / etc. you ever felt doing [what your book is about]?

Make sure you tell your best stories, and sometimes you have to use specific modifiers to remember them. This is very important, so we will repeat it:

Do not tell generic, general stories that have no meaning.

The more honest and emotionally intense the story, the better.

Once these are all plugged in, we should have the logical flow of the chapter. All that remains is to make sure you don't miss anything in the actual interview.

What Is Support?

Support is just some fact or set of facts that helps you remember what it is you want to talk about in that section.

How to create support: In many cases, everything you have above will be enough. This is why support is optional.

But in some cases, you may need a prompt in order to remember everything you want to say in response to a question. This is especially true for things that include lists, details, or very open-ended questions. In other words, support is useful when the answer isn't something that you'd be comfortable explaining off the cuff.

Simply include some short, to-the-point notes to ensure that you cover all the ideas you want to cover in the book. No need to explain things in detail, just a prompt to double-check that it's all been covered.

CONCLUSION

Here's the thing about conclusions: not all books need them. But you should have one. Why?

Because a clear summary of your points is possibly the best thing you can do to not just deliver value to the reader, but also make the book memorable, which helps you sell more books (through creating value for the reader, which creates word of mouth).

That's why we, as a general rule, want our author clients to restate the thesis from the introduction, and then summarize each main point in the clearest, most concise way possible. Give the reader an easy-to-understand and repeat summary of your book to leave with.

This gives the author a chance to pan out once again to the bigger picture—that they initially established in the introduction—and to really drive home the overall lesson they are trying to convey.

What Is a Call To Action, and Why Use It?

But with some books, you might want to go even further here and end the conclusion with a "call to action."

With the call to action, the author usually adopts a different tone, not just more explicitly inspirational but also framed as an *imperative*. The underlying message of the call to action is: *now that you have all the tools, go out there and use them!*

Some authors may feel uncomfortable including such a direct appeal to readers. The approach can be at odds with their usual professorial manner. But a call to action doesn't have to come across in a superficial pep-rally way. It can be whatever you want it to be, whatever feels natural.

The goal here is to spark excitement in the reader and spur them to action. But we're not just looking for hollow words of encouragement. The more specific and reflective of your distinct voice and spirit, the better.

In fact, this is an appropriate place to direct readers to specific resources. Keep in mind, you don't want to make it seem like the whole book was a lead-up to a self-serving pitch for your own company or services. But you *do* want to take the opportunity to send off the reader in all the right directions and equipped with all the information they would need.

READ IT OVER

When you are finally done mapping out the content of each chapter, look over your entire outline. Does it follow a clear internal logic? A successful outline should be able to be read and understood clearly as a book in microcosm. In other words, the dots should all connect. All that's left is to flesh out the details.

THE FINAL PRODUCT

This section can be a little complicated to get your head around, and the best way to grasp it is to see a finished outline. If you'd like to see an example, we have made a few samples available at bookinabox.com/resources.

CHAPTER 6

INTERVIEW AND RECORD YOURSELF

Congratulations! You're finished with the hardest part (the outline process), and now you're ready to start with the fun part (the interviewing and recording process).

The point of this part of the process is very simple: you want to get all of your ideas and knowledge about your book topic out of your head and onto an audio recording which will eventually become the first (very) rough draft of your manuscript.

Why do it this way instead of writing it out in the conventional way?

Because the conventional way of writing a book doesn't work for anyone except professional writers.

It's just too hard, too daunting, to stare at a blank page (or screen) day after day. This is literally called the "blank page problem" and it's a real and serious one. The blank page problem is simply the fear and procrastination that comes with not understanding what to do in order to turn your ideas and wisdom into a book.

Unless you're a professional writer, you don't know where to start, how to proceed even if you do start, or whether or not your writing is any good. You get lost in the details of the act of writing, **which is a completely different cognitive skill than thinking or speaking.**

Think about it this way: you can be an amazing world class race car driver, and literally not have any idea how an engine works, and no one would think twice about that. The job of the driver is to drive the car, not build the engine.

The same thing is true for writing. Your job is to have ideas and wisdom that are valuable to other people, not learn how to write about them. They are completely different skills.

This is the realization that we came to that ultimately created Book In A Box: writing is uncomfortable and foreign to most people, but speaking is very comfortable and people enjoy sharing their ideas by talking about them.

We've helped many talented individuals and fascinating thinkers find the comfort and freedom to traverse the difficult path from idea to book—by simply talking. We interview them, draw the wisdom out through words, and then do the rest, so they never have to worry about the friction that writing introduces into the process.

Remember: Having great ideas, and being able to put them into words on a page, are two TOTALLY different things.

As we discussed earlier, most of the great thinkers of history—Socrates, Jesus, Buddha, Malcolm X, Winston Churchill—did not write anything down. They spoke their words, which were written down by scribes.

Now, by adapting the Book In A Box process for the author who is doing it on their own, we retain this spoken model. The only difference is the interviewing (and recording) is either self-performed or performed by someone the author knows, like a friend or colleague or family member.

WHY SOMEONE ELSE SHOULD INTERVIEW YOU

You may think, "Why do I need someone else? Why can't I just record myself talking?"

You can. It is possible.

But trust us, it's not easy to talk at length about your ideas in the way that is needed here. Even the most long-winded among us are prone to mental shortcuts in our speech. We assume far too much knowledge on the part of the reader, and we oftentimes forget basics because we've been doing something so long. Having someone else interview you forces you to elaborate and explicate, and makes you calm down and talk more casually, which leads to a better book.

Think carefully about who you want to help you with this task.

Ironically, it's preferable—with certain exceptions for highly technical books—to call on someone who *doesn't* know the subject matter in and out. You want an interviewer who is interested in the topic, but doesn't already know too much about it.

That way, they'll prod you, but still make sure your words are clear for a layperson. In fact, even if your friend is a brainiac, you want them to "play dumb," so to speak. The goal is for them to get *more* information out of you than they need.

WHAT DO YOU USE TO RECORD THE AUDIO?

In terms of the recording process itself, technology these days makes it incredibly easy. There are nearly an infinite number of ways to record yourself, and a number of services you can use to get that recording transcribed.

We are going to recommend one service specifically, simply because they make everything so simple: Rev.com

They also have an app you can download on your smartphone. You simply talk into your phone, hit save, and then send it to be transcribed. The cost is $1 per minute, which is standard in the industry.

If this is not possible, we recommend using your internal microphone on your computer, and the software that came with it. Don't make the recording more complicated than it needs to be.

INTERVIEWER INSTRUCTIONS

The purpose of this part of the chapter is to give instructions to *the interviewer*, who we assume will be someone you know, and not you. Open up the book to this page and give it to them to prepare for the interviews.

(At the end, we'll have a set of best practices if you are interviewing yourself that are in addition to the other instructions.)

Staying with the outline is crucial

Interviewing your friend using the Book In A Box method is different than the way a journalist would interview a subject.

You're interviewing to turn your friend's spoken words into content, not just to get the information.

It's crucial to try to stay in sync with the outline. If you stay with the outline as you ask questions, then your friend's answers will generally be in order in the audio recording. This allows them to easily sync up the audio transcription and the outline, which will make editing substantially easier.

If you don't stay with the outline, and just allow your friend to haphazardly jump from random thought to random thought, you might get great material out of them, but when it comes time to put it in the right order and into a book, it will be a mess.

Make sure your friend explains everything completely

If you were interviewing your friend just so you could understand their points, you could do it very quickly. You're smart and you understand things quickly, and it's tempting to tick the box and move on to the next section.

It's easy during the interviews to think, "Yep, got it, let's move on," but when it comes time for writing, your friend will appreciate having the text transcript of their explanation to work from.

But that's not the point of the interview. Your goal in this outline is to get a full, complete explanation out of them—way more than you probably personally need—so that when they sit down to write out the book from their audio transcription, everything is there. The book needs to have enough information to explain the concepts to uninformed people as well as informed people.

It makes things easier, and results in a better book. Even if you're capable of extrapolating the point of what they're saying, it's worth having it on the recording so that the detailed explanation comes through on the transcript. So be sure to ask "Why?" and "Can you explain what you mean by that?" or "Can you be more specific?" often.

Make your friend feel comfortable

The most important part of your interviewing role is to get your friend talking freely. Loosen them up with some small talk, and if necessary, remind them that:

1. There's no pressure since all of this will be heavily edited, so don't try to filter their thoughts to talk like a finished book.

2. More content is better than less, so it's okay to be repetitive; just cover each answer thoroughly.

3. Feel free to explore any tangents when they're feeling in flow (it's your job to bring them back to the outline if it gets off course).

Be interested

Another way to make your friend comfortable and get them warmed up is to encourage them at the beginning, and act very interested in their story and their information. As you well know, everyone likes talking to an engaged audience.

Of course, it's ideal if you *actually are interested*, which is why we encourage authors to find smart friends who want to learn what the author is explaining. Usually it only takes a few words of encouragement to get most people off to the races.

Let your friend speak

The other side of the "being engaged" coin is to not talk over them. All it does is break up their flow. Once they are warm and talking well, they only need minimal interruptions.

It's tempting to add your own input when you have an interesting idea or to cut off your friend when they are being repetitive. Don't. You're reducing the chances that they stumble upon a gem. Many authors need to say the same basic thing over and over in different ways to find the right phrasing. This is normal and natural.

Start with simple questions (or pretend you're an eight-year-old)

The best place to start is with questions that are very simple, open-ended ones. Questions like "Why did you do it that way?" or "How exactly did you do that?" or even "What was the purpose of that?" create a large opening for the author to fill.

Yes, they are simplistic, but that is the point—you want to get all the information possible out of the author.

In all seriousness, we have found that pretending you are an eight-year-old is a great way to get in the mindset to ask these types of questions. Obviously you should not literally act like a child, but it's crucial to get into what the Buddhists call "beginner's mind" and forget all of your assumptions. When they are making assumptions, don't be afraid to ask obvious and simple questions that a child would ask to get the right information out of them.

When you are new to something and not self-conscious about your knowledge (like an eight-year-old would be), you aren't afraid to ask simple, basic questions.

In fact, "Why?" is the best question you can ask in most cases. If you ask that three or four times in a row, you can often get to a place in your friend's reasoning where you're going to understand more of what they think and why, and you'll be able to record the evidence of that thinking to put in the book.

Doing this over and over—asking simple, straightforward questions that force your friend to lay all of their thinking out in the open—helps avoid mistakes, unpacks assumptions, and makes conclusions seem reasonable and correct.

Get the best stories by asking about specific trigger events

Don't let your friend just be general. Ask for specific stories. The best way to get specific stories out of authors is to ask about specific events.

For example, don't say, "Why did you become an entrepreneur?" That will usually only get a broad, generic answer that doesn't get into specifics.

Instead, say something like, "Tell me about the day you decided to become an entrepreneur." That question will bring your friend back to the day she decided to start her company, and she'll tell you the story about how she couldn't pay rent, so she had to sell something online, but there was no place to sell handcrafted goods, so she started her company.

By asking about specific events that triggered important changes in their life (e.g., "tell me about the day"), you push your friend to recount the specific incident that created the decision, not the rationalized story they have constructed afterwards.

That's the way to get stories. Ask them about the one interaction, the day they had to stop, the worst, the first, the best, the one time. Questions that can get at specific stories:

Tell me about the time when...

Tell me about the day when...

Tell me about the moment you realized...

Tell me the story of...

When was the first time you ever [insert activity]? What happened?

What was the first / best / most memorable time that you [insert activity]?

Can you give me an example of a time that you [insert activity] that didn't work?

What day did you decide to [insert activity]? What happened on that day?

Ask for examples, details, and specific step-by-step instructions
When your friend makes a broad claim or statement, ask for a specific example.

For instance, if they say, "I made 50k in one week," follow up with, "Can you explain to me how you did that? What were your exact steps?"

Or another example is if they say, "You can change your life and live your passion and purpose," then your first question should be, "Okay, how exactly would I do that? What is my first step?"

There are an infinite number of ways to use this method to get the right information out of the head of the author. Here are some question formats that work well:

If a stranger were going to do [repeat topic], what's the first thing you'd tell them to do? Where should they start? What should they do today?

How would I do that?

Can you give me an example that your readers could relate to?

Can you explain what you mean?

Can you tell me one story as an example of what you're talking about?

Can you tell me one time you did this?

What were the steps that got you from...to...?

Steer into difficult emotions, not away from them

Famed entrepreneur, radio journalist, and producer Alex Blumberg says it better than we can:

> *"When someone starts talking about something difficult, when they get unexpectedly emotional, your normal human reaction is to sort of comfort and steer away. To say, 'Oh I'm sorry, let's move on.' What you need to do, if you want good tape, is to say, 'Talk more about how you're feeling right now.' It feels like a horrible question to ask. It feels like you're going against your every instinct as a decent human being to go toward the pain that this person is experiencing."* (from Longform Podcast)

At all times, you should think like a potential reader. What would they want to know next? What do they have to know in order for them to understand what your friend understands? What questions will they have, and are you asking them?

Make sure that everything your friend is saying makes sense to you. It's tempting to assume that you're being slow if you don't get it and just smile, nod, and move on. This is wrong. If it doesn't make sense to you, it won't make sense to the reader either.

This means directing your friend back to the aspect of the answer that they are not answering, but that the audience will want to know. Even if you know the answers, it's useful to get the ideas in the author's words.

As Alex Blumberg says again:

> *"Before anyone else can understand the answer, you have to make sure you do. Early in my career, I would play an early draft of a story for an editor, and they would ask, 'When so and so says this, what does she mean by that?' Usually, I wouldn't know. Because I hadn't asked. Even though in the moment of the interview, I'd been a little confused as well."*

This is so, so important:

If you are confused at all, the reader will be too, so make sure you ask for more information, because they can't.

Make small answers big and big answers small

People need to understand the big picture and they need examples. When your friend is talking in the clouds and very theoretical, ask for examples, especially personal ones. We emphasize this—ask for examples—several times, because it is very important.

When they're just telling stories, or just giving you specifics about step-by-step processes, then pull back and ask about the bigger lessons, about how this fits in with the rest of the book and the lessons it's teaching. Even if you already get it, ask them to make the connection explicitly.

Both high level theory and specific details are important to books, so make sure you get the author to provide both.

For memoirs, use questions that elicit emotion and personal reflection

Again, mostly paraphrased from Alex Blumberg:

"You want answers that are real and authentic. To get these sort of answers, you need to ask questions that make people answer your questions using stories or emotion. Questions like:

How did that make you feel? (Sometimes you will need to encourage people here, especially if people aren't used to talking about their emotions.)

If the old you could see the new you... (The transition: What did it mean to them?)

If you had to describe the debate in your head, what would each side say? (This will give voice to the interior drama and break away from the "canned conversation" type answers.)

What do you make of that? (This is a question Ira Glass uses all the time.)

Example of a powerful question: Would you have loaned yourself the money?

Then shut up and let them answer the question."

AUTHOR INTERVIEW INSTRUCTIONS

These are the instructions for you, as the author who is answering these questions.

We've interviewed hundreds of authors through their books at this point, and these are the best practices we have identified.

Relax!

This is the easy part for you. All you need to do here is talk about things you already know. You don't need to worry, you don't need to stress about it, there should just be excitement to talk about a topic you know very well and share it with the world.

Let It Flow.

More is almost always better than less, so please feel free to say everything that comes to mind, especially anything you think is relevant to either answering your friend's questions or to your book topic. Don't worry about phrasing things eloquently, explaining everything perfectly on your first try, or not rambling. Substance matters more than style at this stage, and you only need to worry about getting the substance right.

Later on, you will be working from the transcripts of your interviews to craft the actual book, so always elaborate, even more than you think is necessary. It's much easier to cut words than to add words in places where you don't explain enough.

Tell Stories and Give Examples.

Stories and examples are two of the best ways to make a point. You've done your best to capture stories in your outline, but if a different story ever comes to mind, or another example you thought of, please tell it. It'll make your book better.

Assume You're Talking To an Eight-Year-Old.

You know how kids always ask you "why" and it drives you nuts?

That's actually the job of the interviewer.

Your friend is going to try to pull as much information as they can out of you to go in your book, so they're going to ask you "why" a lot, and they're going to ask things that might seem obvious to you. But the basics are obvious to you because you're an expert. That's why you're writing the book, right?

We want to ensure that you're very clear in explanations, and that you make no assumptions about what your audience knows. It is actually an empirical fact that when people are in the mindset of talking to a totally inexperienced audience (i.e., an eight-year-old), that they give their best, most clear explanations.

We promise you won't come off as condescending or simple. It's much easier for you to "smarten up" a written explanation than to "dumb it down" if it's over the head of the audience or assumes too much.

And if you feel like you're being too obvious, always remember this quote by cartoonist, animator, and activist Nina Paley:

"Don't be original; be obvious. When you state the obvious, you actually seem original."

Have Fun!

Have fun talking about and explaining your field of expertise to your friend. This is your field, so let your excitement and passion come out in your interviews. That will come through in your manuscript, and make your book better.

SKIP THIS IF YOU CAN: INTERVIEWING YOURSELF

We highly recommend you find a friend, family member, loved one, or even someone you've hired to interview you. We cannot recommend that enough.

But we recognize that this isn't always possible, for various reasons. If you absolutely must interview yourself, here are some basic tips. Note that these are in addition to the advice for both the interviewer and the interviewee listed above.

Your questions should already be written out ahead of time, so use them.

Your outline should be formed with questions, and this does two important things. First, it forces you to create an objective list of questions to answer, and second, it gives you the impression you are being interviewed and will prevent you from skipping steps or explanations. Make sure to say these questions out loud and then answer them, as if this is a conversation, and don't just skip to explaining.

Create a reader avatar in your head, and speak to them.

Remember how we focused so much time on figuring out who your audience is? This is so your book will appeal to real people who might really be interested in buying it.

Well, the same thing that is true for positioning needs to be true for the writing. Create an avatar in your head of who the ideal audience is for this book, and then pretend that you are literally talking to them, both as you create questions and answer them. If you can picture a real person you know who fits that mold, that'll make this even easier.

Anticipate what this reader will be most interested in, what they would want to know next, and what questions they would have.

Be honest with yourself: Does everything you're saying make sense to you or are you fudging it with fancy words, etc.? If something doesn't 100% cohere or hang together for *you*, the author, it definitely won't for others.

Be as thorough as humanly possible—even if it seems ridiculous—with the details of your instructions or inquiries. Make sure not to gloss over any steps or rungs in the ladder leading up to your conclusion, even if they seem trivial or self-evident, because the reader won't understand it unless you do. Apply equal energy and rigor to backing up your big ideas with detailed, concrete examples and scrupulous analysis. Again, always focus on connecting the dots.

Go much longer than you think you need to, but give yourself breaks. Even with someone interviewing you, it may be a challenge to keep the interview going as long as is needed. Push yourself beyond your comfort zone. For a final book of 40,000 words, you should be aiming for six to eight hours of interview recording. For 50,000 words, up to ten hours may be needed.

Obviously, you won't be able to do this all in one sitting. It is important that you divvy out the length and make sure to get enough interview material for each chapter. If the outline specifies that the book be broken into, say, three or four parts, tackle each part as its own interview.

Relax and take your time. There's no pressure to be eloquent or say things perfectly. Nor is there any harm in repeating yourself. The goal is just for you to talk through your ideas out loud, to get all of the ideas out of your head and on paper.

CREATE YOUR ROUGH DRAFT

Once you get the transcript of your audio recording from the transcription service, then you will start the process of "translating" that audio transcript into book prose.

This is the closest thing you'll do to conventional writing in the process, but it's not *really* writing. It's actually closer to translating.

What's great about doing it this way is that, like we talked about earlier, you're not facing the "blank page" problem. You never have to sit down and figure out how to not only get your ideas down, but also structure them and refine them, all at once. This process allows you to break it out into easily achievable steps.

FIRST, GET ORGANIZED

Now that you have your transcript, your first order of business is to take that master document and organize it into easily workable chunks.

You do this by cutting and pasting each part (or chapter) into its own separate Word file. The entire book is far too unwieldy at this point to try to do all in one place. You'll feel overwhelmed.

You should know how many different documents you'll need, using the outline as your guide. For example, if your book has an introduction, eight chapters, and a conclusion, then you should end up with ten different files.

Usually, the individual transcriptions corresponding to each chapter should run anywhere from 3,000 to 5,000 words. These are easily manageable chunks to put in one Word document.

When you get the audio transcript, follow these steps:

1. Open up all the new documents.

2. Title each one with the title of the chapter.

3. Copy and paste the outline sections from each at the top.

4. Put in the entire audio transcript for each chapter below that.

This way, you have the structure on the top to always remind you of what your basic point is, and the text below, so it makes it very easy for you to do the next step.

"TRANSLATE" THIS AUDIO TEXT INTO BOOK PROSE

Now that everything is organized, you're going to "translate" your audio text into book prose.

This is not as challenging as original writing, since you've already recorded your ideas on audio and had them transcribed. The words and ideas are there. It's also not pure editing because you will need to rewrite it in most cases.

There are a number of ways to do this, but there is one process that has tended to be most effective for us and our professional editors. It's counterintuitive, but the trick is to go slowly in order to finish more quickly. These are the exact steps we recommend going through for each chapter:

1. Read through the outline for the chapter in order to refresh your memory about exactly the point the chapter is making.

2. Read through the transcript quickly, to recall exactly how you made all your points.

3. Go through one paragraph at a time, read it, and then *rewrite the paragraph.*

We recommend you go paragraph by paragraph, rewriting each one above (literally on top of) the transcription of the same passage.

Some people prefer to do it side-by-side, in two separate Word documents, which is fine too.

The point is you need to physically type your new chapters, paragraph by paragraph, and not just edit the existing chunks of raw transcription.

Why not just edit the transcription directly? Because writing this way is MUCH easier than editing your transcription into writing that reads well on the page.

There's a tendency to want to turn off your brain and use exactly what you say in the transcription, verbatim. This leads to the need for a LOT of editing, and ends up making the process pretty painful.

You'll soon see that transcribed audio is not English. It's very far from what you'll wind up with ultimately. Attempting to edit it will drive you crazy. It's much better to read and absorb the spirit of what each paragraph of transcript is trying to say, and then start fresh with sentences that make sense on the page.

This is essentially translating from one medium, audio, to another, book prose. You'll also see that not everything in the transcript is worth keeping—and so instead of cutting things out, you simply won't rewrite those parts.

Of course, there will be places where you can almost exactly use your words from the transcript. But spoken text tends to jump schizophrenically from point to point, and it reads very differently than it sounds, so trying to bridge those gaps can be awkward.

Instead, look for the points you are making, and *rewrite the content based on those points.*

Think of it this way: The purpose of the transcript was to lay out all the ideas in the right order, so you always know what to say next. The purpose was not to do the writing for you.

Note: In some cases, this may include adding content that isn't in the transcript. Some ideas require some expansion to connect properly. And you may need to add transitions or connections that aren't part of the transcript. This is totally fine, of course. They're your ideas, after all.

Once this is done for all the paragraphs, do a quick read-through of the chapter to make sure the flow of ideas makes sense and the concepts are well explained. And of course, feel free to move paragraphs around as necessary.

If this gets hard, and it will, just keep going. This is where it's easy to give up. You'll regret it if you do.

Again, don't worry about being perfect, as you're going to come back and do a full edit later. This is just getting to the rough draft stage. Just get something down that you can come back to and perfect later.

THE SPECIAL PROBLEM OF THE INTRODUCTION

The meat of your book should be pretty easy to write. It's just you explaining things you know, telling stories, and talking about what you have talked about many times.

The hardest part of your book to write will be the introduction. We actually recommend that you do the introduction *last*, after you've done the rest. This will make it much easier to do the intro.

How To Think About Introductions

Most authors think the purpose of the introduction is to lay out and explain everything they will talk about in the book. That is boring and wrong.

The *actual* purpose of a good introduction is to engage the reader and make them want to read the book. It should be framed more as an interesting sales pitch rather than an informational piece (though it does serve both purposes).

As we discussed in Chapter 5, you need to generally do three things in the introduction:

1. Hook the Reader (what is interesting about the book?)

2. Show Them Pain and Pleasure (explain orientation material)

3. Tell Them What They'll Learn (make thesis statement)

This is a simple formula, and virtually all the best books you've ever read have an introduction that follows this exact process. Here's how you can do it:

Step 1. Hook the Reader (Attention Material)

From *the first sentence*, the author should hook the reader into the book. This means literally beginning the book with a hook line, even if the reader doesn't understand how the line is relevant to the book.

For example, in James Altucher's bestselling book *Choose Yourself*, he begins with these lines:

> *"I was going to die. The market had crashed. The Internet had crashed. Nobody would return my calls. I had no friends. Either I would have a heart attack or I would simply kill myself."*

What does this have to do with the topic of the book (finding success)? And why does James want to kill himself?

I have no idea, but after that beginning, I'm interested and I'm going to keep reading to see what he does. (It actually gets even better after that and you should read the book. Full disclosure: James was a client of our old publishing company and we love him.)

Though the first sentence must be good, the rest of the page and initial story must do the same thing. Starting with an attention grabber—a short story, example, statistic, or historical context that introduces the subject in a way that is interesting and exciting—will engage the reader and compel them to read more, and help lead into the rest of the material.

How To Find Hook Material

Remember: *It may not be easy to see what the hook should be.*

If nothing jumps out, look through the clarification material and ask yourself a few questions:

What is the most interesting story or claim in this book?

What sentence or fact makes people sit up and take notice?

What is the intended audience going to care about the most, or be most interested in or shocked by?

Then, you need to find a way to start the introduction with any of those points, preferably in a way that is interesting, reverses some common idea, or makes the reader take notice in some way.

In fact, many authors wait until their book is at the rough draft stage to finalize what they will use as hook material. If you do this, look for sentences or stories or claims or other statements that jump out at you. The attention material will probably be difficult to identify if you think about it directly, but you can see it by noticing when you personally react to something, or when you notice someone else reacting.

Step 2. Show Their Pain and the Pleasure (Orientation Material)

Once you have the reader's attention with hook material, then the introduction should show why the information in the book matters to them and why they should be paying attention. You do this by orienting them to the material you are about to give them. This means you explain to them why they should care about what you are about to tell them in the book, and how it relates back to the emotions they felt from the hook.

But this is *not about just giving the reader simple information*. It's not enough to list facts and figures. No one pays attention to that. People pay attention to stories, especially stories that resonate with their personal pain and conflicts, and solutions that provide relief and pleasure.

The orientation material should not just be factual, but also personal, and should start by showing the reader the massive pain that accrues from not taking the advice or lessons in this book. Pain induces action.

For example, if you were an author writing a book about how to drive traffic to a website, you need to ask yourself:

"What's an example of how my business suffered when it didn't have traffic to its site?"

Once you've established the pain, then the orientation material should show them pleasure that comes from taking the action. Show them why the results are so amazing and the goal is worth the pain.

In the same example, you could ask yourself something like, "Tell me about something you can do now because you have so much traffic."

Example:

In J.R. Little's book *Listen* about marketing and data—and specifically about how traditional branding and one-way messaging is being replaced by hyper-targeted "listening" to customers in digital and social spaces—the orientation material shows readers that old-style conventional marketing is not working anymore. Companies using it are failing, and marketers with those techniques are losing their jobs.

J.R. then showed what was working (the advice he puts forth in the following chapters, which is adopting a new data-centric approach) and some examples of how these techniques are transforming their businesses for the better (by being able to truly meet their customers' needs and desires).

Step 3. Tell Them What They'll Learn (Thesis Statement)

The introduction should end with a very clear and concise statement of what the reader is going to learn in the book. There are many authors who like to be subtle about this, or "bury the lede."

Do not do this.

Clarity is the key to non-fiction, and your job is to make sure your wisdom is clearly understood by the reader. Make sure that your thesis statement is so clear and simple that even a seventh grader could identify and understand it. You are telling the audience, *here is how you are going to do this, I'm going to walk you through it, step by step by step, until you understand how to do it.*

Another thing to watch out for is trying to accomplish too much with the introduction. Yes, you want it to achieve all of the goals outlined above. But you still want to keep it as concise and streamlined as possible. Nothing turns off a reader more than an introduction that never ends.

Once you get them excited about what they're going to learn, which is the point of the introduction, your job is done. They want to dive in, so end the intro and start the book.

EDIT YOUR BOOK

Congrats! It feels amazing to get through the first rough draft, and you should congratulate yourself and take some time to rest and relax. The hardest part is over, and now you have a real book of your ideas in your hands, even if it is rough.

When we say take some time to rest and relax, we're actually very serious. Set the entire thing aside for at least a week, ideally two weeks. This will give you a fresh perspective when you come back and begin the final edits.

THE TWO-STEP EDITING METHOD

We recommend a two-step editing process:

1. **Read Aloud:** Read the manuscript out loud—preferably to another person.

2. **Manually Edit:** Make changes directly in the document.

We'll explain both processes.

READ ALOUD EDITING

We start with an editing process that's not commonly taught, but is a secret trick of numerous bestselling authors.

You read your manuscript out loud, and mark changes as you go.

This sounds crazy, *but it works*. Paul Graham explains very well why in his essay, "Write Like You Talk."[6]

Okay, so written and spoken language are different. Does that make written language worse?

If you want people to read and understand what you write, yes. Written language is more complex, which makes it more work to read. It's also more formal and distant, which gives the reader's attention permission to drift.

You don't need complex sentences to express complex ideas. When specialists in some abstruse topic talk to one another about ideas in their field, they don't use sentences any more complex than they do when talking about what to have for lunch. They use different words, certainly. But even those they use no more than necessary. And in my experience, the harder the subject, the more informally experts speak. Partly, I think, because they have less to prove, and partly because the

6   http://paulgraham.com/talk.html

harder the ideas you're talking about, the less you can afford to let language get in the way.

If you simply manage to write in spoken language, you'll be ahead of 95% of writers. And it's so easy to do: just don't let a sentence through unless it's the way you'd say it to a friend.

The reason that reading your manuscript out loud works so well is because you will catch dozens of things you would have otherwise missed. Like Paul says, hearing yourself speak forces you to notice bad or strange phrasings—even if you don't why it's off, you know it's off.

Basically, if it's something you would say out loud, then it usually reads clearly on the page. If it's something you would never say to another person, it tends to not read as clearly.

How To Do Read Aloud Editing

We don't recommend that you do this reading off your screen (though you can). We recommend you print out each chapter, and read it aloud, to another person, off of that page.

As you read, you will naturally ask yourself these questions:

"Does this sound the same way I'd say it to someone face to face? Does it feel right to me?"

You (and the other person) will inevitably hear errors, phrasings you want to change, sentences that sound off you want corrected, etc. Mark any clear mistakes you see, or places you want to possibly edit, with a pencil.

If you "feel" something is off, and aren't sure how to change it, that's fine—just mark it the first time through. The first time reading it, you just want to hear the problems, so you can go back and fix them on the page later.

Why do we recommend starting with read aloud, instead of starting with the more conventional manual editing?

The biggest problem we find is that authors will sit with the manuscript for months on end, procrastinating their start and fretting over tiny details. Starting by reading out loud gets you immediate progress and good momentum.

MANUAL EDITING

Once you've read the manuscript out loud, marked the changes, and done one full revision pass, then stop thinking about it for a few days. Give yourself at least 2-3 days away from the manuscript to clear your mind.

We are serious about this; it makes a huge difference. If you obsess over the manuscript for days on end, without giving yourself time away, you won't do as good a job at revisions.

Now that you know it sounds good and reads well, you have one job:

Make sure the book says exactly what you want it to say.

1. As you read every **sentence**, ask yourself these basic questions:

- *What point am I trying to make in this sentence?*
- *Is it clear?*
- *Is it as simple as possible (without losing meaning)?*
- *Is it as short as possible (without losing meaning)?* (**Note:** You can break this down even further, with questions like *Are there unnecessary words that could be eliminated without any effect?* If so, there's no reason for them to be there, so cut them. *Are there phrases that serve no purpose other than draw out the sentence, like "in essence" and "basically"?* If so, cut them.)
- *Did I leave out anything necessary to understanding my point?*

2. Apply the same basic questions to the **paragraphs**. At the end of each paragraph, ask yourself these basic questions:

- *What point am I trying to make in this paragraph?*
- *Is it clear?*
- *Is it as simple as possible (without losing meaning)?*
- *Is it as short as possible (without losing meaning)?*
- *Did I leave out anything necessary to understanding my point?*

3. Then apply it to the **chapters**. As you finish each chapter, ask yourself these basic questions:

- *What point am I trying to make in this chapter?*
- *Is it clear?*
- *Is it as simple as possible (without losing meaning)?*

* *Is it as short as possible (without losing meaning)?*
* *Did I leave out anything necessary to understanding my point?*

We mean this literally—ask yourself these questions, each time.

Yes, this is tedious, but if you do this exercise, you'll find that you can not only cut a lot of fluff out of your book, you can also make your book sharper and more refined, and you'll be able to really home in on what you are trying to say, and nail it.

(By the way, we adapted these instructions from George Orwell's essay *Politics and the English Language*, which are probably the best editing instructions from arguably the greatest writer of the 20th century.)

Some other editing notes and things to keep in mind as you edit:

Openings matter: In the same way that the book's introduction is vital, pay special attention to your chapter openings. Each chapter should have a clear goal that is stated directly for the reader (in the same way the overall book does in the introduction).

Transitions are key: Think of your writing like a mathematical proof. In math, there is no obscuring with pretty language. If you are attempting to make a mathematical statement, one theorem or axiom has to set up the next. In your manuscript, you want each chapter to connect to the following one, but you also want each section within a chapter to connect. Ultimately every paragraph, and even every sentence, should serve a purpose.

Rewriting is okay: It's okay if you need to *rewrite* certain passages again. That's part of the editing process.

Focus on content: At this point, don't focus too much on spelling, grammar, punctuation, etc., but that all comes later in the publishing process. Of course fix any obvious problems you see, but the proofreader's job is to fix those.

Beware of word repetition: You shouldn't use the same word over and over again in the same paragraph or on the same page, especially if it's an uncommon word (obviously, you're going to repeat words like "the," etc.). Make your thesaurus your friend. But at the same time, don't substitute in words that sound obviously thesaurus-y. It feels unnatural, and the reader can tell.

Watch out for clichés and useless adverbs: Clichés are so ingrained that we don't notice them. In fact, sometimes we congratulate ourselves for writing something that sounds writerly when in fact it's just a cliché. If you're writing a book, say, on income inequality, you may be tempted to throw around the phrase "abject poverty." But before you do, think about what you're saying. Are you just using those words together because they're frequently combined, or do you really just mean to say "poverty"? In fact, even if you do mean to use "abject," you should replace it with a less common synonym like "extreme" or "wretched."

SHOULD YOU LET FRIENDS GIVE FEEDBACK ON YOUR MANUSCRIPT?

It depends. Like everything else, it really depends on what you want.

Other people can definitely give you very helpful feedback on your book. The hard part is ensuring you only get feedback from *the right people.*

Before we explain why you need to be very careful about who you solicit feedback from, think about another extension of the previous example we used:

If your car broke down because of an engine problem, would you ask a race car driver—one who has driven a lot but doesn't fix engines as his job—to look at your car and tell you what's wrong with it?

Maybe, but that's not the best thing to do. The best thing is to take your car to a mechanic. Why? Because he's an expert at actually fixing engines, not driving a car.

You should look at your book that way as well. If you want to show your manuscript to someone to get feedback, it should generally be a person from one of these two groups:

1. People who are experienced writers or editors, or

2. People who are in the exact audience you want your book to reach.

Let's break down each category:

1. Experienced writers or editors

This is obvious. Someone who has a lot of experience in writing and editing can almost certainly help you with your manuscript and give useful feedback.

But remember, many people *vastly overestimate* their experience and ability in these areas. Many people think they are skilled writers or editors, when in fact they are not at all.

This is why at Book In A Box, we have a rigorous testing process before we even begin to work with freelance editors, outliners, and publishing managers—even if they are employed full time as writers or editors, we don't assume they are skilled. We want to see their work, and we judge their ability by the quality of their work. What happens as a result of these tests? We reject about 75% of the freelancers who apply to work with us, all of whom have legitimate writing or editing experience. That should tell you the general quality of the "experts" out there.

We bring this up only because we've seen many authors give their manuscript to a friend who claimed to be a "great" writer, only to see that friend give truly awful notes that left the author confused and hurt, and ended up creating lots of problems with the book.

Here's the hard reality of book feedback: *most people have NO IDEA what they are talking about,* especially with regards to books and writing, and getting feedback from those people is harmful. **So be careful.**

2. Someone in the audience for your book

This type of feedback can be very helpful, but you need to be careful to ask the right questions.

If your book is about—for example—how to build an app business, and you give it to two friends who are trying to build app businesses, their feedback could be very helpful. They could tell you what really helped them in the book, what parts they wished had more content, and where they got confused or lost. That sort of feedback tends to be very valuable.

One thing to remember about those people, though, is this quote from famous author Neil Gaiman:

> *"When people tell you something's wrong or doesn't work for them, they are almost always right. When they tell you exactly what they think is wrong and how to fix it, they are almost always wrong."*

His point is a different version of the one we made above. Very few people are good enough at writing or editing to actually know how to do it well. They may know that your book isn't working for them in some way, and that critique should be listened to. But their ideas for solutions are probably bad, because they have no experience actually solving writing problems.

If someone in your audience says something isn't working for them, listen to their comments, but use your own ideas and knowledge to fix the problem. No one knows your book and your subject matter better than you do.

FINISH THEM!

Always do one last read through of your manuscript, make your last minutes changes, and then move on.

We see this all the time at Book In A Box. We finish the rough draft and give it to the author for their edits and feedback. And they spend six months with it, not really making substantive changes, but instead get lost in details, like fretting over very small word choices. We have to almost pry the book out of their hands so that we can finish it, even though they don't really have anything left to change.

This can be driven by many different forces such as perfectionism, fear of publishing, fear of success, fear of failure, etc. There will always be more to work on, more to change, more to perfect. But that thinking will kill you.

What causes it doesn't really matter. What matters at this point is that you stop editing and put the book out. There is no good in recording your wisdom if you never share it.

If you have reached this point, and are editing too much, then you need to stop. We can literally write a whole different book about this subject, but we're going to simply say this:

At least one person, and probably many more, want to learn what your book can teach them. You have an obligation to yourself and to your audience to stop editing and put the book out.

Give your wisdom to them, even if it's not perfect. They want and need it.

If you are planning to actually use this method to write your book, stop reading right now, and go start writing. The rest of the book is irrelevant and useless until you actually have a finished manuscript that you are happy with.

Seriously. STOP READING.

Go work the steps and write your book.

PUBLISH
YOUR BOOK

PUBLISHING 101

Writing your book is the hardest part of publishing your book. But what happens after you've finished writing? How do you go from finished manuscript to published book?

Answering that question, in a clear, detailed, and actionable manner, is what this section of the book is about. At the end of this book you will know exactly how to do every step necessary to professionally publish your own book.

Part 3 of this book should have two major takeaways for you:

1. Publishing a professional book yourself is not easy.

2. Publishing a professional book yourself is absolutely doable, if you follow these steps.

There are things in life that require a lot of artistic skill and involve dealing with uncertainty. Book publishing does not have to be one of them. It's just a series of steps. You deal with them one at a time, methodically and systematically, and then the book is done.

That's partially the reason why people get overwhelmed when they're publishing a book; it feels like there's this mish-mash of all these different steps and they don't know where to start and they don't know what's important, and how to prioritize.

The point of this book is to get rid of that uncertainty and to show book creation as a linear series of steps with an explanation of precisely how you take each one. All that is left for you is to do it.

Important Note: But before you can worry about publishing, *you must have a finished manuscript.* If you're reading this chapter, we're assuming you have one done.

If you don't have a finished manuscript yet, *you're not ready for the instructions in the upcoming pages.* Close this book and go do that first.

If you have a finished and locked manuscript, then let's get going!

Secondary Note: If you are really confused about books and book publishing, this book is probably *not* the right place to start. This is a quick and simple step-by-step guide on exactly how to you can professionally publish your own book once you have a finished manuscript and you've decided to self-publish, it does not explain the entire landscape of book publishing.

If you need more background information about book publishing, then visit this link and read this blog post on our site: How To Understand The Book Publishing Landscape[7]

That blog post was written for people who do not really understand books and book publishing, and want a lot more background information before starting on their book publishing journey. It is long and comprehensive, and has answers to questions like these:

- How does book publishing work? What are the most important things to know?
- What is "self-publishing"?
- What is "traditional publishing"
- Why does the difference matter?
- Should I self-publish or traditionally publish my book?
- How do I get a traditional publishing deal?
- How do I evaluate traditional publishers?
- What is professional vs. amateur in publishing, and why does that matter?

TIME TO GET STARTED

If you just do every step necessary, you're only a few weeks from your own professionally published your book. Let's get started!

---

7   http://bookinabox.com/publishing-landscape/

LOCK IN YOUR MANUSCRIPT

Be perfectly clear: when we say you need "a finished manuscript" to start the publishing process, we don't just mean a document that's pretty close to your finished book. We don't mean a file with only a few typos left.

We mean a *finished manuscript.*

Combing your book for edits is fine. It's great, in fact. You want your book to be perfect, and that's important. But it's crucial that you get as much of that work out of the way as possible before starting the publishing process. Adding a paragraph now rather than after the interior layout is finished can mean the difference between a few minutes and *a few hours* of work.

This is NOT hyperbole. Our interior book layout people tell us that, for most authors, about 50% of the time they spend laying out the book comes from the author's last minute changes. Getting your manuscript locked in now translates to literally mean thousands of dollars of savings. It's worth taking the time to proofread thoroughly.

There are two basic methods we recommend to proofread your manuscript before locking it in. The first is to do it yourself (using a simple trick that almost all professional authors do, as we explain below). The second is to hire a professional.

In our experience, your best bet is to do both. Professionals put in the extra time (or hire someone else to do that).

DO IT YOURSELF

There's one trick that separates almost all of the professional authors from the amateurs. It's one of those little things that seems simple and doesn't take too long to do, but for some reason seems too intimidating for many first-time authors: read your full manuscript out loud.

When I was first writing *I Hope They Serve Beer In Hell*, I had teams of proofreaders working through the book. First I proofread it myself, then I had the help of professional editor friends, and finally the publishing company did their copyedits. I didn't think that a single mistake would sneak by, and happily locked in the manuscript.

A few months later I recorded his audiobook, and as I read through the manuscript out loud, I was horrified to find small mistake after small mistake.

Not only did I catch a few typos and other obvious mistakes but, more importantly, I found places where the wording just sounded off. If the words roll off your tongue, they'll also flow smoothly in readers' heads. Because I waited until so late in the process to read it out loud, it was too late to make edits to the book.

Learn from my mistake and *read your manuscript out loud and make your changes before you start the publishing process.*

If you find taking the time to sit and read out loud difficult (and a lot of authors do), we recommend having a friend help you out. If someone is sitting in the room with you, listening as you read through the manuscript, it'll create the social pressure you need to actually do it.

Plus, you'll be sure to truly read out loud and not skim.

(If you want to know how much time to budget for this activity, you can roughly estimate that you'll read 150 words per minute. For a standard 40,000 word manuscript, that should take about 4.5 hours.)

We don't want to waste too much time hammering this point home, but it's seriously important.

Don't skip this step.

HIRE A PROFESSIONAL PROOFREADER

The other method of proofreading that we'd recommend is hiring a professional proofreader or copy-editor.

I know it seems crazy. You've just read through the book out loud, you had your "editor" friends read it, and you're pretty confident there are no mistakes. But you're wrong. There is a lot of data on this, but average people only detect about 60% of errors, and even professionals usually only catch about 80% of errors.[8]

While your out-loud reading will catch a lot of the small, sloppy mistakes and wording issues, there are a whole other set of issues that professional proofreaders are looking for: small grammatical rules that native English speakers often don't even realize exist.

Do you know the difference between an en-dash and an em-dash? Do you end sentences in prepositions? These kinds of mistakes are not life threatening, but they make the differences between a professional book and one that comes across as amateur.

There are a lot of services that offer proofreading. The main distinction is between those services where you submit the manuscript and they manage their proofreading team internally, and marketplaces that allow you to find your own freelancer. The first is simpler, but the second (using marketplaces) tends to be more effective.

Editing Services

If you choose to go with editing services, you'll likely be charged a flat fee. You can ballpark that these options will cost

8   https://www.copyediting.com/error-rates-in-editing/

about $200-400. You'll submit the manuscript, and within a week you'll get back a finished product. Simple.

Here are a few services we've tested and recommend:

- PostScripting (https://postscripting.net)
- Kibin (https://www.kibin.com)
- Scribendi (http://www.scribendi.com)

Marketplaces

The other alternative is to use a marketplace. Most of these options will allow you to list a job for free, and the marketplace will take a percentage of the proofreading costs. The proofreaders will usually work on a per hour or per word basis ($20-30 per hour and 0.75-1 cent per word are normal), but some will be open to charging a flat fee as well. The total cost should be similar to the prices above.

Here are a few marketplaces we've tested and recommend:

- Upwork (https://www.upwork.com)
- People Per Hour (http://www.peopleperhour.com)
- MediaBistro (http://mediabistro.com)

The real benefit of using a marketplace instead of a service is the direct engagement you get with the proofreader. Not only will you be able to choose someone who seems best suited for your project (and who has been rated well by past clients), but you'll be able to convey extra information to them that might be useful in their proofreading work.

Once you've found the right proofreader, you'll need to assign them the job and work with them. We spoke to our team of professional proofreaders to gather up feedback on what they need out of a job assignment, and this is the advice they came up with:

1. **Define the Role:** As one of our proofreaders said, "Proofreading is rarely just proofreading, no matter what the client calls it." There's a lot of responsibility that can be put on a proofreader, and it's important to be clear about what that responsibility is.

    Traditionally, a proofreader's task is specifically to find any errors, like typos, grammatical mistakes, and spelling mistakes. However, it's not uncommon (because they're the last line of defense against a faulty manuscript being released) for proofreaders to take on more responsibility.

    We like this, so we actively encourage it. Our proofreaders know that their role is really "proofreading plus" and includes copyediting and fact checking as well.

2. **Explain the Audience:** Not every book is written in the Queen's English, nor should they be. For a proofreader to know what to edit and what's intentional, it's important for them to understand the audience for the book and the message it's trying to convey.

    This can be as high level as whether or not profanity is

okay, or as specific as the country of origin to make sure that the sayings and spellings are correct.

If you are reading this book, you may already know we put an emphasis on understanding your audience and goals before starting with writing. This is why: It informs every decision in the writing and publishing process.

3. **Point Out What Needs Work:** Often (although not always) there are issues that you know will come up. For example, we recently worked on a book that was written in such a way that it jumped back and forth between past and present tense. We went through and fixed this problem, but it was worth mentioning to the proofreader that this was an issue we'd run into, and to pay special attention for these mistakes. Other times, you just ask the proofreader to work through it carefully with their usual processes.

The same goes if you have a tendency to make sloppy typos, or misuse a certain type of punctuation, or any other clues as to what they might be looking for.

FINISH THE PROOFING PROCESS

Once the proofreader is done, they should send you back a Word document with Track Changes. This is the industry standard, and it's worth confirming with proofreaders **before** hiring them that they'll be tracking the changes for you.

When you receive the document you should expect to find hundreds of small tracked changes. Most of these will be obvious mistakes that you're happy to quickly accept, but some may be phrasing recommendations or questions about pieces that are unclear. Be sure to go through all of these changes and make your own decisions about what should be implemented and what shouldn't.

READY TO PUBLISH?

At this point, you should have a manuscript that you're confident enough to lock in.

We should note that you'll probably never be 100% confident that your manuscript is ready to go. No writer is. But at some point—generally after all of these steps—there is nothing else left for you to do other than lock it in and put it out. Don't waste weeks or months trying to get it from 99.9% perfect to 100%. It's impossible. Recognize when diminishing marginal returns have set in, and move on.

READY TO MOVE ON?

→ Complete your manuscript

→ Read your manuscript out loud

→ Hire a professional proofreader

Once you're confident with your locked in manuscript, it's time to move on to the next phase of the process: choosing your title and subtitle.

CHAPTER 11

CHOOSE YOUR TITLE

The title of your book is by far the most important book marketing decision you'll make. Shockingly, there's little good guidance out there on the right way to think about titling your book. The few blogs that address this decision offer advice that has some fundamental problem:

- *Trite:* "Go with your gut!"
- *Superficial:* "Browse bookstores for ideas!"
- *Actively harmful information:* "Don't spend too much time on it."

They're all wrong.

Just like companies that spend millions on naming new products, and blogs that spend hours testing different titles for their posts, **you should spend serious time and energy finding the right book title.**

This is a very important decision, one you need to think about and get right to ensure your book has the best possible chance of success.

WHY DO BOOK TITLES MATTER?

The title is the first piece of information someone gets about your book, and it often forms the reader's judgment about your book.

Let's be clear about this: A good title *won't* make your book do well. But a bad title will almost certainly *prevent* it from doing well.

Based on loads of empirical research and our decades of experience in the book business, we have a pretty clear picture of what happens in the mind of a potential reader when he or she is evaluating a book.

They consider these pieces of information about a book, in this order (assuming they come across it randomly in a bookstore or browsing on the Internet):

1. The title of the book

2. The cover of the book

3. The back cover copy (the book description copy, if it's online)

4. The flap copy (or the reviews, if it's online)

5. The author bio (depending on where it's located)

6. The book text itself (or they use the "see inside" function to read a few paragraphs)

7. The price

How is the title first? Well, in most cases, the title is the first piece of information the reader sees or hears about your book—even before the cover in most cases. This is why **getting your title right is possibly the most important single book marketing decision you'll make** (even though most people don't think about it as marketing).

The iconic example of the importance of a book title is the title change that led to an obscure book becoming a #1 bestseller. In 1982 Naura Hayden released a book called *Astro-Logical Love*. It bombed.

She then took the exact same book, changed a small amount of the content, and re-issued it with a different title, *How to Satisfy a Woman Every Time...and Have Her Beg for More!*

That book became a massive cultural phenomenon and #1 bestseller. Same book, same content, just a different title. The take-away for you is simple and clear:

Spend time figuring out the best possible title for your book, because it will determine a large part of what people think about your book, and thus, your book's success.

THE FIVE ATTRIBUTES OF GOOD BOOK TITLES

A good title should have all of these attributes:

1. Attention grabbing

2. Memorable

3. Informative (conveys what book is about)

4. Easy to say

5. Not embarrassing or problematic for someone to say aloud to their friends

6. The right length

1. Attention Grabbing

This should be pretty obvious. There are a million things pulling on people's attention, and you need a title that stands out. A bad title is one that's boring or seems boring.

There are many ways to grab attention; you can be provocative, controversial, exciting, make a promise, etc. The point is your title should make people stop and pay attention to it. Here is what #1 best-selling author Tim Ferriss says about titles:

> "*The 4-Hour Workweek also bothered some people and was ridiculed by others, which I took as a positive indicator. It's not accidental that Jay Leno parodied the book on-air—the title lends itself to it, and that was by design. You can't have strong positive responses without strong negative responses,*

and beware—above all—the lukewarm reception from all. 'Oh, that's nice. I think it's pretty good,' is a death sentence."

2. Memorable

This is not the same thing as grabbing attention (even though many people think it is). It's much easier to get a reaction out of someone, and then be forgotten, than it is to get a reaction *and be memorable.*

Remember, a book title is not only the first thing a reader hears about your book, it's the one piece of information that a reader has that leads them back to the book itself. If your book is recommended to them by a friend, and they can't remember the title, then they can't go find it in a bookstore or on Amazon. Bestselling author Scott Berkun says it well:

> *"Often [the title] is all a potential buyer ever gets to see, and if they can draw interest the book crosses its first of many hurdles in the improbable struggle of getting noticed. But titles only help so much. Most people hear about books the same way they hear about new bands. Or new people to meet. A friend or trusted source tells them it was good and it was called "X." The title at that point serves as a moniker. It's the thing you need to remember to get the thing you want to get and little more."*

3. Informative (conveys what the book is about)

This is the least crucial aspect for fiction books, but very important for nonfiction. The title, including the subtitle, should give the reader some sort of idea of what the book is about.

People aren't going to do your work for you; the easier you make it on them to understand the subject, the more likely you are to draw in the people who could find your book interesting.

A good test is this: *if you were to tell someone the title of your book at a party, would they have to ask what it's about?*

If so, that's probably a bad title.

Also, don't out-think yourself on your title. A title that is very clever or somewhat unclear signals that the book is for people who immediately understand the word or phrase—which makes people who don't get it right away feel stupid, and thus less likely to buy the book.

By using a word or phrase that is either not immediately understandable by your desired audience, or doesn't convey the point of the book, you are putting a huge obstacle in front of your success.

4. Easy to say

This is closely tied to being understandable, but not the exact same thing. Obscure or difficult-to-pronounce words are killers for titles. Tongue twisters and hard-to-say phrases reduce the likelihood that people will engage with the book or say the title out loud to other people.

This is a concept called cognitive fluency.[9] Simply put, it means that people are more likely to remember and respond

---

9   http://www.uxmatters.com/mt/archives/2011/07/how-cognitive-fluency-affects-decision-making.php

favorably to words and phrases they can immediately understand and pronounce. We don't want to go too far into the psychological literature here; the point is this: Don't try to be too sophisticated at the risk of becoming obscure. It will only hurt your book.

5. Not embarrassing or problematic for someone to say

It's a basic fact of human psychology—people don't like to feel stupid or socially awkward. If a book title is hard to pronounce, or more importantly, if it's a phrase that sounds stupid when said out loud, that makes them far less likely to buy it, and they definitely aren't going to talk about it to other people.

One of the most important things to think about when picking your book title is how well it facilitates word of mouth. Really, what you're doing is thinking about *how people will feel* about saying this book title out loud to their friends. Does it make them look smart or stupid?

The worst possible title is one that makes someone sound stupid after saying it out loud. For example, if the book title is something like "Why Racism Is Great," no one is ever going to tell their friends about it. It doesn't matter how good the book is, because they have to then face the scrutiny of why they even bought that book in the first place. Social context doesn't just matter some, it matters a lot.

A great example is Ryan Holiday's book *Trust Me, I'm Lying*. He originally wanted to call it *Confessions of a Media Manipulator* (which became the subtitle), but was talked out of it by his publisher. What happened? The title is catchy, but also immediately brands him as a liar—even though the point of the book is how the media system is set up so that it forces EVERYONE to lie, and he hates that and wanted to change it.

But think about the implications of saying this title out loud—you are, unconsciously of course, calling yourself a liar. It resulted in a lot of confusion and negative implications about the book that could have been avoided with a clearer title (this is also partly an issue of #3, making sure the title conveys what the book is about).

6. The right length

The goal is to have the main title be as short as possible—no more than five words—and have the subtitle offer the context and include important keywords.

There are a lot of reasons for this, but generally speaking, the longer the title, the more confusing it is and the harder it is to remember. Both are bad.

THE BOOK TITLE TEST

Here's a great test as to whether or not you have a good book title: imagine one of your readers talking about your book at a party to other people. If you can see them confidently saying the book title aloud, and the people listening nodding and immediately either understanding what the book is about based on that (and perhaps a sentence or two of explanation), or asking for further explanation because it sounds interesting, then you've got a good title.

If you imagine *any other reaction than this one*, you need to re-think your title, and probably change it.

Remember, so much of book marketing boils down to word of mouth, and word of mouth is all about people signaling things to other people. You want your book title to inspire and motivate the right people to talk about it, because it lets them signal the right things to their friends.

DOES YOUR BOOK NEED A SUBTITLE?

It depends. If you're doing a nonfiction book then yes, probably so. If you're writing, fiction, no, probably not. But in both fiction and nonfiction, you can make good case for the opposite, so it depends.

Books need a subtitle if it's necessary to contextualize the subject alluded to in the main title. Typically, the subtitle tells the reader some combination of what the book's central premise is, who the book is for, and what promise the book delivers on or need it meets.

Some examples where subtitles help contextualize the title:

1. *The 4-Hour Workweek: Escape 9-5, Live Anywhere, and Join the New Rich*

See how the title hooks you by being interesting, and the subtitle explains the premise? Very well done.

2. *Daring Greatly: How the Courage to Be Vulnerable Transforms the Way We Live, Love, Parent, and Lead*

It's a bit long, but the same thing is going on here; the subtitle contextualizes and frames the title, which is clear and easy to understand and say.

3. *Kitchen Confidential*

This originally had a subtitle, *Adventures in the Culinary Underbelly*, but it was later dropped. No subtitle needed on this work of nonfiction, because the meaning is fairly clear, especially when paired with a picture of a chef on the front (and because it became very famous, which helps).

4. *The Looming Tower: Al-Qaeda and the Road to 9/11*

This is an example of a book where the subtitle is very important. That title could mean many things, but the subtitle quickly signals what the book is about and who it's for.

SPECIFIC STEPS TO FINDING A GOOD BOOK TITLE

Step 1. Understand Your Book and Your Goals

Obviously your book goals (building a brand, selling copies, etc.) will determine what type of title you pick. If you want to build a brand out of your nonfiction book, then your title options are much different than if you want to publish a novel with a whimsical title.

Let's examine all the functions your book title can serve, and the places it potentially could be used, before we walk you through the precise process of thinking up title ideas.

Functions a Book Title Can Serve

- To sell the book to readers in some way
- Establish the author's authority on a subject
- Identify the Amazon/B&N listing
- Start a line of books
- Branding for a company, author, conference, or course materials
- Advertising/marketing the book
- Used in speeches, slides, or other in-person activities
- Used in reviews, blog posts, articles, etc.
- It's something the author has to say in all his or her press appearances
- Become a defining part of an author's future bio
- Decorate the cover
- Used on T-shirts, flyers, or other promotional material

The point of this whole list is simple: **Know which of these goals are for your book, and make sure your title can serve those goals.**

For example, if your goal is to build a brand, you need to make sure your book title is your brand. Dave Asprey's first diet book is called *The Bulletproof Diet*, because that's his brand: Bulletproof. The book is about selling everything around the book, not just the book itself.

Whereas a memoir is about catching people's attention with the title, and making them curious. A great example is Dave Eggers memoir, *A Heartbreaking Work of Staggering Genius*. The title is so audaciously overstated that it makes you think, "Is this guy kidding?" and you want to know more about him and the book. It catches your attention, just like a memoir title should.

Step 2. Brainstorm a Bunch of Potential Titles

This step is simple: **Spend at least a few days writing down every single title idea you can think of.**

Telling someone to brainstorm is like telling someone to "be creative," meaning that it's not an easy thing to describe. That being said, we will will list every possible way we know of to find a good book title, complete with examples (remember, these techniques are not just for your main title, they will be the basis for your subtitles as well).

These are just some best practices for coming up with title ideas. We don't know of any titles that can incorporate all of these, but they are all potentially effective ways to go with titling books:

1. Use clever or noteworthy phrases from the book: This is very common in fiction, and can work well with novels. It also works well with nonfiction books where the concept of the book can be summed up quickly or with one phrase.

Examples:

+ *The Black Swan*
+ *Lecturing Birds on Flying*
+ *I Hope They Serve Beer In Hell*

2. Use relevant keywords: For nonfiction especially, search matters. You want to make sure that when someone searches for the subject or topic of your book, it will come up on Google and Amazon. But it's a balancing act, because you don't want to sacrifice the authenticity of the work for what looks and feels like a search string query.

If you are unsure of this, go look on Amazon and see how often subtitles and titles use additional keywords to attract more search engine traffic.

Examples:

- *The 7 Habits of Highly Effective People: Powerful Lessons in Personal Change*
- *Mindset: The New Psychology of Success*

3. Make a promise of a benefit: Some of the best titles promise to help readers achieve a desired goal or get some wanted benefit. They specifically call out to an end result that people want:

Examples:

- *How To Win Friends and Influence People*
- *Getting Things Done*
- *Think and Grow Rich*

4. Be simple and direct: Some of the very best titles are just basic statements about what the book is. There is nothing wrong with this; it can work well, especially for strictly instructional books.

Examples:

- *Getting Past No*
- *Steve Jobs*
- *The Power of Habit*

5. Target an audience: As we told you, people use titles to judge if the book is for them. Part of helping people understand this can be directly targeting them in your title. You can target specific audiences by naming them, or by describing their characteristics. This works especially well if you have a series of books, and then do versions targeted to specific niches.

Examples:

- *What to Expect When You're Expecting*
- *Physics for Future Presidents*

6. Offer a specific solution to a problem: This is very popular in the self-help and diet spaces. Basically, you tell the reader exactly what problem your book solves in the title. This is sort of similar to the promise of a benefit, but not the exact same thing; a benefit is something additive, like being sexy. A solution to a problem takes away something negative, like losing weight.

Examples:

- *Man's Search for Meaning*
- *6 Ways to Lose Belly Fat Without Exercise!*

- *Secrets of Closing the Sale*

7. Use numbers to add credibility: Specifics like numbers add credibility and urgency to your titles. They can provide structure for your information, or they can make hard things seem easier. Specificity enables people to engage the idea in a more concrete way, and gives bounded limits and certainty on time frames as well.

Examples:

- *The 48 Laws of Power*
- *The Five Love Languages: The Secret to Love that Lasts*
- *The 21 Irrefutable Laws of Leadership*

8. Pique the reader's curiosity (but withhold the answer): Using statements that seem to be impossible, unusual contrasts, or paradoxes can make readers curious about what is in the book. The idea is to make a claim or statement that seems a little farfetched or fantastical, but promises delivery. This is very popular now with headline writing on sites like Upworthy and ViralNova.

The iconic recent example of this with books is one we already mentioned: *The 4-Hour Workweek*. Everyone wants to know how to work four hours a week, since it seems impossible. So you pick up the book to see what that guy is talking about.

Examples:

- *Networking Is Not Working*

- *10% Happier*
- *Who Moved My Cheese?*

9. Use metaphors or symbols associated with the themes in your book: Humans think in symbol and metaphor. Using these powerful devices can help you create a title that really resonates.

The iconic metaphor-based series is the *Chicken Soup for the Soul* series. The title signals the warm, nurturing feeling that is associated in our culture with chicken soup, which is what you get when you are sick, and connects it to something else—stories that nurture your soul.

Examples:

- *Lean In*
- *The Untethered Soul*

10. Use alliteration: Alliteration is just using the same letter at the beginning of all or most of the words in your title. This makes things easier for humans to remember.

Examples:

- *The Mighty Miss Malone*
- *A Storm of Swords*
- *The Pop-Up Paradigm*

11. Alter a popular phrase: This is pretty common in book titles and tends to work pretty well—taking a famous phrase and altering it in a way that makes sense for your book. This works because it's close to something people know, but not exactly the same thing.

Examples:

- *The War of Art*
- *Assholes Finish First*

12. Use slang: Slang can work really well, especially if it's used in a way that is non-intuitive but also novel.

Examples:

- *Ain't Too Proud To Beg*
- *No Mopes Allowed: A Small Town Police Chief Rants and Babbles about Hugs and High Fives, Meth Busts, Internet Celebrity, and Other Adventures*

13. Try cliché formats (or reversing them): There are a ton of book-naming tropes that some people say to avoid. We don't think you should avoid them if they make sense for your book, or if you can reverse them in novel ways. Any of these work well:

- The Art of [TOPIC]
- The Myth of [TOPIC]
- Confessions of [TOPIC]
- How to [TOPIC]
- The Joy of [TOPIC]
- The End of [TOPIC]

Examples:

* *The Art of Racing in the Rain*
* *The Myth of Male Power*
* *Confessions of an Economic Hitman*
* *How To Train Your Dragon*
* *The Joy of Sex*
* *The End of Science*

14. Consider coining a phrase or new word: This is very helpful, especially if you want to create a brand or company or extended product line out of your book. The problem with this is that it's not an easy thing to do. Many authors try to create new words; few succeed, so try this sparingly.

Examples:

* *Babbitt*
* *Denialism*

15. Use Amazon/Goodreads/Wikipedia for inspiration: If you're feeling stuck, you can always go look at how other books are named.

* Wikipedia's list of best-selling books of all time[10]
* Goodreads' list of best book titles[11]
* Amazon's current best-selling books[12]

10 http://en.wikipedia.org/wiki/List_of_best-selling_books

11 http://www.goodreads.com/list/show/276.Best_Book_Titles

12 https://www.amazon.com/best-sellers-books-Amazon/zgbs/books

16. Try random title generators: Look, I'm not going to tell you these are great ways to find book titles. But sometimes people get desperate, and this is something you could try if you run out of other options:

Some sites to check out:

- http://www.kitt.net/php/title.php
- http://www.fictionalley.org/primer/title.html

17. Use copywriting manuals for ideas: If you are truly stuck and cannot think of anything, read some books about copywriting. They are not specifically about book titling, but copywriters have to understand the sell triggers for people, and they will give you tons and tons of examples. These are three of the best out there:

- POP!: *Create the Perfect Pitch, Title, and Tagline for Anything*
- *The Ultimate Sales Letter: Attract New Customers. Boost your Sales.*
- *Advertising Headlines That Make You Rich: Create Winning Ads, Web Pages, Sales Letters and More*

Step 3. Pick Your Favorites (and Maybe Test Them)

So at this point you should have a long list of title ideas. If you don't, go back and keep brainstorming until you have at least 10-20. Once that is done, you can move on to the next step, though this is optional: testing your titles.

I cannot emphasize how important this next step is. Everyone has opinions on book titles. **Most of those opinions are stupid and wrong.**

Even people who get PAID to come up with book titles (editors, publishers, etc.) are usually very bad at it.

It's easy to express an opinion about a book title. It's harder to empirically test that opinion with objective data, because that could show your opinion is wrong. Fight the feeling to go with your gut, and use the simple and easy tools that exist to get some data. Don't let ego or creative preciousness get in the way of the best marketing decision. We often find that what we think will be the most popular title lags back in third or fourth place.

Here's one of the keys to testing your titles: test both the main title and subtitle, and test them in many different iterations. Usually what you'll find is most things test about the same, while there will be one thing that clearly tests better as a title, and another that clearly tests best as a subtitle.

This is a great piece[13] about the step-by-step process of using Google AdWords to test a title.

If you have a large audience already, you can also use SurveyMonkey.[14]

For real customer feedback, I recommend using PickFu.[15]

---

13 http://itrevolution.com/phoenix-project-google-adwords-title-subtitle-testing/

14 https://www.surveymonkey.com/

15 https://www.pickfu.com/

I would also recommend Google Survey.[16] This is real market testing of real people, and can be done fairly cheaply.

Step 4. Listen To the Results

I know this might seem ridiculous to say, but *listen to the results you get.*

Or at the very least, if you know you aren't going to listen to the results, then don't run the test. Getting data just to ignore it is a huge waste of time.

Step 5. Check the Results Against Your Goals

Here's the rub with testing, and potentially the reason to avoid it: it can be wrong, especially if you run it wrong.

Remember the example I gave above about Ryan Holiday and his title, *Trust Me, I'm Lying*? Well, that one tested the best out of 6 potential titles.

But not so fast. The problem is that he ran the test in such a way that it was not well representative—most of the results came not from Google AdWords, but from surveys he gave to his friends and readers who knew him well. Biased results.

Ryan relied too much on the data, and not enough on the knowledge *around the data*, and a careful consideration of how that title would be interpreted by other people, especially by those in the media. He didn't really think about his goals, whether that title served all of his goals, and most importantly,

---

16   https://www.google.com/insights/consumersurveys/home

how the title sounded to people who didn't know him when they heard it out loud at a cocktail party.

Step 6. Make Sure This Title Is Not Already Popular

No, you cannot copyright titles. Technically, you can call your book "To Kill a Mockingbird" or "Lord of the Rings" or even "The Holy Bible."

That being said, copying a popular books makes it VERY hard for your book to stand out, and pretty much guarantees a lot of negative reviews from people who are not getting the book they expected to get.

READY TO MOVE ON?

→ Brainstorm a long list of potential titles

→ Choose the best title from your list

→ Confirm that this title matches your goals and isn't already popular

Now that you have your book title (and subtitle, if you have one) confirmed, it's time to write your book description.

WRITE THE PERFECT BOOK DESCRIPTION

After the title and the cover, the most important marketing material for your book is the description.

The book description goes on the back cover (for paperbacks) or the inside flap copy (for hard copies) and right below the price (on Amazon).

It's crucial that this short paragraph be right. There are so many examples of how a change in book descriptions led to huge changes in sales, it's incredible authors don't spend more time getting it right.

One of our favorite examples of this is Louise Voss and Mark Edwards' novel, *Killing Cupid*. Despite a nice cover and good reviews, it wasn't selling as many copies as it should have. Edwards dove into the competition, analyzed their book descriptions, and completely revamped the book's description. Sales doubled...*within an hour.*

This isn't uncommon. In many cases, the description is the factor that solidifies in the reader's mind whether the book is for them or not. If you get it right, the purchase is almost automatic. If you get it wrong, very little else can save you.

In this chapter, we will walk you through how to write a great book description and include some examples of authors who did it well, and those who didn't.

HOW TO WRITE YOUR BOOK DESCRIPTION

There are three basic factors you need to consider before starting your book description:

1. **Word Count:** Brevity matters. On average, Amazon bestsellers have descriptions that are about 150-250 words long. Most descriptions are broken into two paragraphs (although some are kept at one, and some run to three).

2. **Simple Writing:** Keep the writing simple and clear, using short sentences. You don't want anyone to struggle to comprehend what you're trying to convey because you've strung too many ideas together in one long run-on sentence.

3. **Write as the Publisher, Not the Author:** This will probably be obvious to you, but the book description should

always be in a third person objective voice, and never your author voice.

Apart from those three basic principles, book descriptions can vary widely, but here are the best practices that we've seen that get the most effective results:

1. Understand It's an Ad, Not a Summary

Don't think of the book description as a synopsis. It is an advertisement. It is not meant to summarize your book. It is designed to make people want to read your book. You want them to take action and buy it. Think of it like a trailer for your book.

So many authors want to put everything about their book in this section. Resist that urge. Remember what you are looking for in a random book description—a reason to read the book.

How do you give someone a reason to buy it? You state the problem or question your book addresses, you show that you solve or answer it, but you leave a small key piece out. This piques the interest of the reader and leaves them wanting more (examples below).

2. Use a Great First Line

Grab them from the first sentence. People are always looking for a reason to move on to the next thing. Don't give it to them.

If that first sentence isn't right—or worse, if it's wrong—you can lose the reader immediately, and then it doesn't matter what the rest of the description says. Make the first sentence something that forces them to read the rest of the description.

3. Make It Personal and Relevant

Make the description personal, and clearly explain why anyone interested in the subject the book addresses needs to read it. Done right, this creates an emotional connection by describing how the book will make the potential reader feel after reading it. Or even better, what the reader will get out of reading the book.

Will it make them happy or rich? Will it help them lose weight or have more friends?

Be clear about the benefits; don't hint at them. You are selling a result to the reader, not a process (even though your book is the process to get the result, people care about the result, not your process).

4. Don't Hide the "What" or the "How"

Explain exactly what the book is about in clear, obvious terms. Do not make the reader struggle to understand what the point of the book is, or how you get the reader there.

For some books it's not enough to write a compelling ad with important keywords; sometimes you need to give readers a sense of where this book is going and how it gets there. This is especially true for prescriptive books (how-to, self-help, motivational, etc.). People like to understand the "how" as well as the "what," especially if it's something new or novel.

This being said, make sure to leave just enough mystery to

make them buy the book; this is a balance that our examples (below) will show you how to hit.

5. Use Compelling Keywords

It's not enough to be accurate, you need to use high interest keywords that increase the likelihood your book will get picked up in an online search.

For example, if *Sports Illustrated* does a book, the authors not only should mention *Sports Illustrated* magazine in the description, but also the names of the A-list athletes in the book.

Even better, use words that evoke an emotional response on the part of the reader. Don't use "jerk" when "asshole" will work.

6. Bullet Points Are Okay

If it makes sense for what you're trying to convey, use bullet points to list information. They are an effective visual tool that make your description scannable and easily digestible. People like to scan; let them.

7. No Insecurity

Don't compare your book to other books. We see this all the time, and all it does is make the book (and the author) immediately look inferior. Plus, a reader the may hate the book you are comparing yourself to, and you'll lose them.

The only place a comparison makes sense is if you are quoting a very reputable source that makes the comparison itself (and that usually falls in blurbs).

8. Do Use Beneficial References

Don't compare to other books, but DO use what benefits the book does have. If there is an impressive stat to mention (e.g., a *New York Times* bestseller), that will be bolded in the first sentence.

Or if there is one salient and amazing fact about you or the book, that can go in the book description, something like, "From the author of [INSERT WELL KNOWN BESTSELLING BOOK]."

Or perhaps, "From the world's most highly decorated Marine sniper, this is the definitive book on shooting."

9. If You're Struggling, Get Help

We can't tell you how many amazing authors we've had come to us utterly befuddled because they couldn't write their own book description. *This is normal.*

The reality is that the author is often the worst person to write her own book description. They're too close to the material and too emotionally invested.

If this is the case, we recommend asking a friend to help, or going to a professional editor or, even better, a professional copywriter for assistance.

BOOK DESCRIPTION EXAMPLES

Tim Ferriss's 4-Hour Workweek
Forget the old concept of retirement and the rest of the deferred-life

plan—there is no need to wait and every reason not to, especially in unpredictable economic times. Whether your dream is escaping the rat race, experiencing high-end world travel, earning a monthly five-figure income with zero management, or just living more and working less, The 4-Hour Workweek is the blueprint.

This step-by-step guide to luxury lifestyle design teaches:

- *How Tim went from $40,000 per year and 80 hours per week to $40,000 per month and 4 hours per week*
- *How to outsource your life to overseas virtual assistants for $5 per hour and do whatever you want*
- *How blue-chip escape artists travel the world without quitting their jobs*
- *How to eliminate 50% of your work in 48 hours using the principles of a forgotten Italian economist*
- *How to trade a long-haul career for short work bursts and frequent "mini-retirements"*

What Makes It Good?

There are three things that make this description good.

1. It has a great first sentence: Tim immediately tells you why this book matters to YOU—because you can stop waiting for retirement. Who doesn't want to retire now? Okay, I'm interested, tell me more...

2. It has bulleted, specific info: A vague promise is no good if it doesn't deliver. Tim then makes specific promises about

the information in the book, both about things that have happened and things it will teach you.

3. It makes you want to read more: After the contrast of the big broad goal and the specific information, at the very least, any reader is going to keep going into the reviews and other information. You're hooked—you want to know HOW he teaches this.

Nir Eyal's *Hooked*

Why do some products capture our attention, while others flop? What makes us engage with certain products out of habit? Is there a pattern underlying how technologies hook us?

This book introduces readers to the "Hook Model," a four-step process companies use to build customer habits. Through consecutive hook cycles, successful products reach their ultimate goal of bringing users back repeatedly—without depending on costly advertising or aggressive messaging.

Hooked is a guide to building products people can't put down. Written for product managers, designers, marketers, startup founders, and people eager to learn more about the things that control our behaviors, this book gives readers:

- *Practical insights to create user habits that stick.*
- *Actionable steps for building products people love.*
- *Behavioral techniques used by Twitter, Instagram, Pinterest, and other habit-forming products.*

Nir Eyal distilled years of research, consulting and practical experience to write a manual for creating habit-forming products. Nir has taught at the Stanford Graduate School of Business and Hasso Plattner Institute of Design. His writing on technology, psychology and business appears in the Harvard Business Review, The Atlantic, TechCrunch, and Psychology Today.

What Makes It Good?

Three things make this good:

1. **Engaging questions:** Instead of stating a goal, this book asks some fundamental questions that many people are looking for answers to. This immediately catches the interest of potential readers.

2. **Important keywords:** We tend to advocate staying away from buzzwords in your book description, but in some cases—especially business books—the right use of them can work. This is an example of where they work. Words and phrases like "actionable steps" and "practical insights" and "habit forming products" actually work.

3. **Establishes legitimacy:** The description does not deliver much information about how this works aside from vague promises, so to compensate, the author's bio is emphasized. This is important for establishing legitimacy. Names like "Stanford" and "Harvard" signal to the reader that this guy is for real.

Tyler Cowen's *Average Is Over*
Widely acclaimed as one of the world's most influential economists,

Tyler Cowen returns with his groundbreaking follow-up to The New York Times bestseller The Great Stagnation.

The widening gap between rich and poor means dealing with one big, uncomfortable truth: If you're not at the top, you're at the bottom.

The global labor market is changing radically thanks to growth at the high end—and the low. About three quarters of the jobs created in the United States since the great recession pay only a bit more than minimum wage. Still, the United States has more millionaires and billionaires than any country ever, and we continue to mint them.

In this eye-opening book, renowned economist and bestselling author Tyler Cowen explains that phenomenon: High earners are taking ever more advantage of machine intelligence in data analysis and achieving ever-better results. Meanwhile, low earners who haven't committed to learning, to making the most of new technologies, have poor prospects. Nearly every business sector relies less and less on manual labor, and this fact is forever changing the world of work and wages. A steady, secure life somewhere in the middle—average—is over.

With The Great Stagnation, Cowen explained why median wages stagnated over the last four decades; in Average Is Over he reveals the essential nature of the new economy, identifies the best path forward for workers and entrepreneurs, and provides readers with actionable advice to make the most of the new economic landscape. It is a challenging and sober must-read but ultimately exciting, good news. In debates about our nation's economic future, it will be impossible to ignore.

What Makes It Good?

This book description does almost everything right. It quickly but unobtrusively establishes the author's credentials, it immediately states the huge social question it addresses, and it does so in a way that creates an emotional reaction from the reader—questions of equality are highly emotionally charged.

It then spends two short paragraphs laying out the context of the debate over economic equality and then tells you exactly what the book will tell you, without giving its thesis away. This description almost forces you to read this book.

SOME BAD EXAMPLES

Ben Horowitz's *The Hard Thing About Hard Things*

Ben Horowitz, cofounder of Andreessen Horowitz and one of Silicon Valley's most respected and experienced entrepreneurs, offers essential advice on building and running a startup—practical wisdom for managing the toughest problems business school doesn't cover, based on his popular Ben's Blog.

While many people talk about how great it is to start a business, very few are honest about how difficult it is to run one. Ben Horowitz analyzes the problems that confront leaders every day, sharing the insights he's gained developing, managing, selling, buying, investing in, and supervising technology companies. A lifelong rap fanatic, he amplifies business lessons with lyrics from his favorite songs, telling it straight about everything from firing friends to poaching competitors, cultivating and sustaining a CEO mentality to knowing the right time to cash in.

Filled with his trademark humor and straight talk, The Hard Thing About Hard Things is invaluable for veteran entrepreneurs as well as those aspiring to their own new ventures, drawing from Horowitz's personal and often humbling experiences.

What's Wrong with It?

This description is bad because—based just on this description—the book seems somewhat bland and boring. If I don't know anything about Horowitz before I read that description, what in there makes me want to know more?

Nor does it really tell me anything about the substance of what he says in the book, and it substantially undersells both Horowitz's prominence and the resonance and importance of the book's message.

And who cares that he likes rap? What does that matter to me, the reader?

Compare this with the description for Tyler Cowen's book above; it explains who Cowen is and why I should care, it tells me what he says, applies the book to my life, and shows me exactly why I need to care about what he wrote.

The irony is that having read both books, I can tell you that Horowitz's is just as good, if not *better* than Cowen's. But you would never know this from comparing the descriptions.

Douglass Rushkoff's *Coercion: Why We Listen to What "They" Say*
Noted media pundit and author of Playing the Future Douglas

Rushkoff gives a devastating critique of the influence techniques behind our culture of rampant consumerism. With a skilled analysis of how experts in the fields of marketing, advertising, retail atmospherics, and hand-selling attempt to take away our ability to make rational decisions, Rushkoff delivers a bracing account of media ecology today, consumerism in America, and why we buy what we buy, helping us recognize when we're being treated like consumers instead of human beings.

What's Wrong with It?

Short descriptions are great, but this is too short to even tell me what the book says. This is an example of overselling, without doing it right. Look at the descriptions, "devastating" "skilled analysis" and "bracing account"—this description sounds like he's doing what he says he's warning us about: selling without substance. In no place does this description connect the reader to the issues in the book in a way that is engaging or compelling.

READY TO MOVE ON?

→ Write your book description

→ Ensure that your description fits the criteria above

With your book description completed, you can now start your author bio.

CRAFT YOUR
AUTHOR BIO

Unless you're one of the household name authors (e.g., Steven King, J.K. Rowling, or Malcolm Gladwell), then you have to assume that most of the people thinking about buying your book will not know who you are.

So how will they learn about you?

The author bio. It goes on your book, your Amazon page, and most marketing material, and it's the way most people will first hear about who you are.

Even though very few authors think about it, and few writing or publishing guides talk about it, your author bio will impact sales, frame your reputation, and often determine what media coverage you get.

How does this work?

"Author reputation" is consistently cited as one of the main factors that influence book buying. If you can establish yourself as an authority on your book topic, readers will be much more inclined to buy your book, read it, and regard you the way you want them to. People considering spending their disposable income on your book are looking for a reason to do it or not, and a great bio helps them do it (while a bad bio often will stop them).

Furthermore, if you are like most authors and want your book to help create more business for you, or establish your credibility or authority on a subject, often the author bio is *more important* that what's actually in the book.

How could this be? The sad but true reality is that more people will read your author bio than your actual book. It takes a long time to read a book, but it's very easy to make a snap judgment based on a short paragraph—and most people do that.

This is doubly true for media. Most people in media work very hard under tight deadlines. They don't have time to read long books or long, meandering pitch emails. But a good author bio cuts right to the point by telling them: *this is a person who is important and I need to pay attention.*

HOW TO CRAFT YOUR AUTHOR BIO

Writing about yourself as an author is typically a task that most writers shy away from, but writing an effective author bio doesn't have to be so painful. In fact, with a few simple steps you can have an effective bio that not only will impress interested publishers, but also help sell your book.

Less is usually more when it comes to author bios, and you want to make sure you do (and don't do) the following:

1. Demonstrate your authority and credentials on the subject of your book (but don't overstate them)

2. Include things that build credibility or are interesting (without going overboard)

3. Mention your website and any books you have previously written (but don't oversell them)

4. Use relevant names, if they are appropriate (without name dropping)

5. Keep it short and interesting (without leaving anything important out)

You notice a pattern here?

Good author bios walk a line. They avoid being boring and uninspiring, and they avoid being ridiculously over-promotional and arrogant.

Now we'll break each category down, and then give you some examples:

1. Demonstrate your authority and credentials on your book subject (but don't overstate them)

Whatever your book is about, it's important that you establish your credentials in that area. For example, if you're writing a diet book, mention any sort of professional degrees or training, your own weight loss success, or other things that clearly signal your authority and credibility on weight loss.

If you struggle with what to say about yourself, remember that you want to make clear why you're credible and professional (as opposed to an unknown, untrusted source), i.e., *why the reader should listen to you.*

For some types of books and authors, this is harder to do. If there is no clear way to signal direct authority or credentials—for example, a novel or a book of your life's stories—then don't make up things or try to "invent" authority. Focus on the other parts of the author bio.

2. Include things that build credibility or are interesting to the reader (without going overboard)

In your author bio you'll want to include some things you've accomplished in your life, especially if you don't have direct credentials and authority in the book subject matter. This will help your audience understand why they should spend their time and money reading what you've got to say.

If you have something about you or your life that is unusual, even if it's not totally relevant, you should still consider putting it in your bio. For example, if you were a Rhodes Scholar, or you started a major national organization, or won a national championship in ping-pong—whatever. The point is to show the reader that you have done things that matter, that you are an effective person, even if those things don't matter specifically to the book.

If you are lacking credentials or exciting accomplishments, you can always put in your passions and interests. Anything that you enjoy doing, writing about or consider a hobby, especially if it is relevant to the book topic.

That being said, do NOT ramble on and on about things that the reader doesn't care about. Cramming too much into your bio can show insecurity, and bore the reader. Put yourself in your reader's shoes, and ask yourself, "Does this fact really matter to anyone but me?"

3. Mention any books you've written, and your website (but don't oversell them)

If you've written other books, especially on that subject, make sure to mention them. If they're bestsellers or won awards, even better. If you've won multiple awards and you are finding that listing them all is becoming tedious, aim for brevity instead. Simply writing "John Smith is an award winning author whose works include…" is more than enough to show your readers you know what you're doing.

If you have a website, a longer bio page, or anything else that helps promote your brand, then make sure you include it at the bottom of your bio (assuming this meets your goals). Again, you don't want to brag here so just be humble and simply put something like "Find out more about John at www.

johnsmithwriter.com." It's simple and has a clear call to action.

4. Use relevant names, if they are appropriate (without name dropping)

Yes, name dropping can be really off-putting if it's done wrong. But there is a right way to do it.

For example, if you are relatively unknown, you can say something like, "The woman who Seth Godin called 'the most important writer of our time' reveals to you the secrets of..." This way you are trading on Seth Godin's reputation, and establishing your credentials at the same time (assuming he actually said this).

Also, if you've worked for or with very well-known people, name dropping is not seen as bad; it's seen as an effective signal to the reader of your importance and ability. What matters is that there is a reason that you are using someone else's name that make sense, and is not just a gratuitous name drop.

5. Keep it short and interesting (without leaving anything important out)

While your readers are interested in finding out more about you, they don't want to get bored or listen to arrogant braggadocio about how great you are. If your bio is too long, or too full of overstated accomplishments and awards, it will turn your readers off and actually make you look less credible.

Typically if you keep your bio under 250 words you're going to be okay. Anything longer than that means you've gone on too long about your accomplishments, your personal life, or both. Cut it down to the most important things.

IF YOU CAN'T WRITE ABOUT YOURSELF, HAVE FRIENDS HELP YOU

Most people, especially writers, have a hard time writing about themselves. Often, the author bio is the most difficult part of the marketing process.

If you are unsure about whether your author bio seems either incomplete, or too arrogant, run it by a few friends for feedback. It's always easier for your friends to praise you and see the amazing things you do.

REMEMBER: YOUR BIO GROWS AS YOU GROW

Treat your bio as a living document. Just because you've written it once does not mean it's finished. As you grow and change, so too should your bio.

Also, remember that if you are writing for different genres or different topics that some of your accomplishments and past works will be more relevant to your readers than others. It's not a bad idea to tweak your author bio for each new work you release.

EXAMPLES OF DIFFERENT AUTHOR BIOS

Good Balance: Tim Ferriss

Tim does lean aggressively into the idea of listing all the cool things he's done and noteworthy outlets that have talked about him, but still makes his bio interesting and relevant to the reader of his books:

Timothy Ferriss is a serial entrepreneur, #1 New York Times best-selling author, and angel investor/advisor (Facebook, Twitter, Evernote, Uber, and 20+ more). Best known for his rapid-learning techniques, Tim's books—The 4-Hour Workweek, The 4-Hour Body, and The 4-Hour Chef—have been published in 30+ languages. The 4-Hour Workweek has spent seven years on The New York Times bestseller list.

Tim has been featured by more than 100 media outlets including The New York Times, The Economist, TIME, Forbes, Fortune, Outside, NBC, CBS, ABC, Fox, and CNN. He has guest lectured in entrepreneurship at Princeton University since 2003. His popular blog www.fourhourblog. com has 1M+ monthly readers, and his Twitter account @tferriss was selected by Mashable as one of only five "Must-Follow" accounts for entrepreneurs. Tim's primetime TV show, The Tim Ferriss Experiment (www. upwave.com/tfx), teaches rapid-learning techniques for helping viewers to produce seemingly superhuman results in minimum time.

Confusing and Slight Overselling: Cheryl Strayed

Cheryl is similar to Tim, but runs several unrelated things together in a confusing way, and mentions things that no reader would ever care about (e.g., who the director of a movie based on her book is). This same bio could be 25% shorter and much stronger.

Cheryl Strayed is the author of #1 New York Times bestseller WILD, The New York Times bestseller TINY BEAUTIFUL THINGS, and the novel TORCH. WILD was chosen by Oprah Winfrey as her first selection for Oprah's Book Club 2.0. WILD won a Barnes & Noble Discover Award, an Indie Choice Award, an Oregon Book Award, a Pacific Northwest Booksellers Award, and a Midwest Booksellers Choice Award, among others. The movie adaptation of WILD *will be released by Fox Searchlight in December 2014. The film is directed by Jean-Marc Vallée and stars Reese Witherspoon, with a screenplay by Nick Hornby. Strayed's writing has appeared in* THE BEST AMERICAN ESSAYS, *The New York Times Magazine, The Washington Post Magazine, Vogue, Salon, The Missouri Review, The Sun, Tin House, The Rumpus—where she wrote the popular "Dear Sugar" advice column—and elsewhere. Strayed was the guest editor of* BEST AMERICAN ESSAYS 2013 *and has contributed to many anthologies. Her books have been translated into more than thirty languages around the world. She holds an* MFA *in fiction writing from Syracuse University and a bachelor's degree from the University of Minnesota. She lives in Portland, Oregon with her husband and their two children.*

Bad Doctor Bio: Dr. David Perlmutter

This is a long, uninterrupted string of hard-to-process things. Dr. Perlmutter is very qualified, but mentions everything (including medical school awards) which detracts from the overall effect.

David Perlmutter, MD, FACN, ABIHM, *is a Board-Certified Neurologist and Fellow of the American College of Nutrition who received his* M.D. *degree from the University of Miami School of Medicine where he won the research award. Dr. Perlmutter is a frequent lecturer at symposia sponsored by such medical institutions as Columbia University, the University of Arizona, Scripps Institute, and Harvard University. He has contributed extensively to the world medical literature with publications appearing in The Journal of Neurosurgery, The Southern Medical Journal, Journal of Applied Nutrition, and Archives of Neurology. He is the author of: The Better Brain Book and the #1 New York Times Bestseller, Grain Brain. He is recognized internationally as a leader in the field of nutritional influences in neurological disorders. Dr. Perlmutter has been interviewed on many nationally syndicated radio and television programs including 20/20, Larry King Live, CNN, Fox News, Fox and Friends, The Today Show, Oprah, Dr. Oz, and The CBS Early Show. In 2002 Dr. Perlmutter was the recipient of the Linus Pauling Award for his innovative approaches to neurological disorders and in addition was awarded the Denham Harmon Award for his pioneering work in the application of free radical science to clinical medicine. He is the recipient of the 2006 National Nutritional Foods Association Clinician of the Year Award. Dr. Perlmutter serves as Medical Advisor for The Dr. Oz Show.*

Good Doctor Bio: Dr. Benjamin Carson

Contrast this to Dr. Carson, who focuses only on the credentials and status signifiers that the reader would care about and understand, like his specialties and companies he works for.

Dr. Benjamin Carson is a Professor of Neurosurgery, Plastic Surgery, Oncology, and Pediatrics, and the Director of Pediatric Neurosurgery at Johns Hopkins Medical Institutions. He is also the author of four bestselling books—Gifted Hands, Think Big, The Big Picture, and Take the Risk. He serves on the boards of the Kellogg Company, Costco, and the Academy of Achievement, among others, and is an Emeritus Fellow of the Yale Corporation.

He and his wife, Candy, cofounded the Carson Scholars Fund (www.carsonscholars.org), a 501(c)3 established to counter-act America's crisis in education by identifying and rewarding academic role models in the fourth through eleventh grades, regardless of race, creed, religion, and socio-economic status, who also demonstrate humanitarian qualities. There are over 4800 scholars in forty-five states. Ben and Candy are the parents of three grown sons and reside in Baltimore County, Maryland.

High Status and Short: Lynn Vincent

This bio is the perfect "less is more" for an author with a lot of credentials. When you have done what Lynn has done, you can just say it quickly and succinctly.

Lynn Vincent is The New York Times best-selling writer of Heaven Is for Real and Same Kind of Different As Me. The author or coauthor of ten books, Lynn has sold 12 million copies since 2006. She worked for eleven years as a writer and editor at the national news biweekly WORLD magazine and is a U.S. Navy veteran.

High Status But Undersells: Michael Lewis

Contrast this to Michael Lewis, who is a very well known author, but still leaves quite a bit out of his bio that would help many readers understand who he is and why they should care (even Michael Lewis is not famous enough to assume people know him).

Michael Lewis, the author of Boomerang, Liar's Poker, The New New Thing, Moneyball, The Blind Side, Panic, Home Game, and The Big Short, among other works, lives in Berkeley, California, with his wife, Tabitha Soren, and their three children.

Bad: Amanda Ripley

Many authors have different bios on different books (because they leave the bio writing to their publisher, which is a huge mistake). You can see the difference in the author Amanda Ripley. Her bad bio is strangely both boring and overselling:

Amanda Ripley is a literary journalist whose stories on human behavior and public policy have appeared in TIME, The Atlantic, and Slate and helped TIME win two National Magazine Awards. To discuss her work, she has appeared on ABC, NBC, CNN, FOX News, and NPR. Ripley's first book, The Unthinkable, was published in fifteen countries and turned into a PBS documentary.

Good: Amanda Ripley

Contrast that to this good bio, where she comes off as much more of an authority—mainly because her other books are mentioned, as were her awards.

Amanda Ripley is an investigative journalist for TIME, The Atlantic, and other magazines. She is the author, most recently, of THE SMARTEST KIDS IN THE WORLD—and How They Got That Way. Her first book, THE UNTHINKABLE: Who Survives When Disaster Strikes—and Why, was published in 15 countries and turned into a PBS documentary. Her work has helped TIME win two National Magazine Awards.

Good First Person Bio: Charles Duhigg

Personally, I don't think first person bios work well. But some authors like them, as do some readers. The only place they feel appropriate to me as About pages of websites. But of the first person bios I've seen, this is the best.

My name is Charles Duhigg, and I'm a reporter for The New York Times. I'm also the author of The Power of Habit, about the science of habit formation in our lives, companies, and societies.

I've worked at the Times since 2006. Last year, I was part of a team that won the Pulitzer Prize for a series about Apple named "The iEconomy," and before that, I contributed to other series, including "Golden Opportunities" (which received the George Polk Award, the Sidney Hillman Award, and a Deadline Award), "The Reckoning," (which won the Loeb and was a finalist for the Pulitzer Prize), and "Toxic Waters," (which received The Scripps Howard National Journalism Award, the Investigative Reporters and Editors' Medal, the National Academies' reporting award, and others.)

I'm a native of New Mexico and I studied history at Yale and received an MBA from Harvard Business School. Before becoming a journalist, I worked in private equity and—for one terrifying day—was a bike messenger in San Francisco. I have appeared on This American Life, The Colbert Report, NPR, PBS NewsHour with Jim Lehrer, and Frontline.

If you would like to contact me, I would love to hear from you. I'm at charles@charlesduhigg.com.

This is such unnecessary overselling. Rebecca Skloot wrote a major bestseller (*The Immortal Life of Henrietta Lacks*), but she mentions all sorts of nonsense in this bio that no reader will care about. You get the "doth protest too much" vibe from this. Compare this to Tim Ferriss, who also lists a lot but does so quickly and gets out of the way.

Rebecca Skloot is an award-winning science writer whose articles have appeared in The New York Times Magazine; O, The Oprah Magazine; Discover; and others. She has worked as a correspondent for NPR's Radiolab and PBS's NOVA Science-NOW, and is a contributing editor at Popular Science magazine and guest editor of The Best American Science Writing 2011. She is a former Vice President of the National Book Critics Circle and has taught creative nonfiction and science journalism at the University of Memphis, the University of Pittsburgh, and New York University. Her debut book, The Immortal Life of Henrietta Lacks, took more than ten years to research and write, and became an instant New York Times bestseller. She has been featured on numerous television shows, including CBS Sunday Morning and The Colbert Report. Her book has received widespread critical acclaim, with reviews appearing in The New Yorker, Washington Post, Science, Entertainment Weekly, People, and many others. It won the Chicago Tribune Heartland Prize and the Wellcome Trust Book Prize, and was named The Best Book of 2010 by Amazon.com, and a Best Book of the Year by Entertainment Weekly; O, The Oprah Magazine; The New York Times; Washington Post; US News & World Report; and numerous others.

We'll end with one of the worst bios I've ever seen. This is a real bio, pulled of the Amazon page of his recent book. It is over 500 words of preposterously insecure and arrogant crap. I can't imagine reading this bio and not respecting the author LESS afterwards:

Dinesh D'Souza has had a 25-year career as a writer, scholar, and public intellectual. A former policy analyst in the Reagan White House, D'Souza also served as John M. Olin Fellow at the American Enterprise Institute, and the Robert and Karen Rishwain Fellow at the Hoover Institution at Stanford University. He served as the president of The King's College in New York City from 2010 to 2012.

Called one of the "top young public-policy makers in the country" by Investor's Business Daily, D'Souza quickly became known as a major influencer on public policy through his writings. His first book, Illiberal Education (1991), publicized the phenomenon of political correctness in America's colleges and universities and became a New York Times bestseller for 15 weeks. It has been listed as one of the most influential books of the 1990s.

In 1995, D'Souza published The End of Racism, which became one of the most controversial books of the time and another national bestseller. His 1997 book, Ronald Reagan: How an Ordinary Man Became an Extraordinary Leader, was the first book to make the case for Reagan's intellectual and political importance. D'Souza's The Virtue of Prosperity (2000) explored the social and moral implications of wealth.

In 2002, D'Souza published his New York Times bestseller What's So Great About America, which was critically acclaimed for its thoughtful patriotism. His 2003 book, Letters to a Young Conservative, has become a handbook for a new generation of young conservatives inspired by D'Souza's style and ideas. The Enemy at Home, published in 2006, stirred up a furious debate both on the left and the right. It became a national bestseller and was published in paperback in 2008, with a new afterword by the author responding to his critics.

Just as in his early years D'Souza was one of the nation's most articulate spokesmen for a reasoned and thoughtful conservatism, in recent years he has been an equally brilliant and forceful defender of Christianity. What's So Great About Christianity not only intelligently explained the core doctrines of the Christian faith, it also explained how the freedom and prosperity associated with Western Civilization rest upon the foundation of biblical Christianity. Life After Death: The Evidence shows why the atheist critique of immortality is irrational and draws the striking conclusion that it is reasonable to believe in life after death.

In 2010, D'Souza wrote The Roots of Obama's Rage (Regnery), which was described as the most influential political book of the year and proved to be yet another bestseller.

In 2012, D'Souza published two books, Godforsaken and Obama's America: Unmaking the American Dream, the latter climbing to #1 on The New York Times bestseller list and inspiring a documentary on the same topic. The film, called "2016: Obama's America," has risen to the second-highest all-time *political documentary, passing Michael Moore's Sicko and Al Gore's An Inconvenient Truth. In addition, 2016 has risen to #4 on the bestselling list of all documentaries.*

These endeavors—not to mention a razor-sharp wit and entertaining style—have allowed D'Souza to participate in highly-publicized debates about Christianity with some of the most famous atheists and skeptics of our time.

Born in Mumbai, India, D'Souza came to the U.S. as an exchange student and graduated Phi Beta Kappa from Dartmouth College in 1983.

D'Souza has been named one of America's most influential conservative thinkers by The New York Times Magazine. The World Affairs Council lists him as one of the nation's 500 leading authorities on international issues, and Newsweek cited him as one of the country's most prominent Asian-Americans.

D'Souza's articles have appeared in virtually every major magazine and newspaper, including The New York Times, Wall Street Journal, The Atlantic, Vanity Fair, New Republic, and National Review. He has appeared on numerous television programs, including the The Today Show, Nightline, The News Hour on PBS, The O'Reilly Factor, Moneyline, Hannity, Bill Maher, NPR's All Things Considered, CNBC's Kudlow Report, Lou Dobbs Tonight, and Real Time with Bill Maher.

READY TO MOVE ON?

→ Write your author bio

→ Ensure that your bio fits the criteria above

Once you've completed your author bio, you're ready to take an author photo to go alongside it.

TAKE THE RIGHT
AUTHOR PHOTO

This is an important and hard truth that most authors avoid:

Readers will judge you AND *your book based on your author photo.*

Is that fair? Maybe not. Is it reality? Absolutely (and you probably do it with books, as well).

Why do people do this—even though most people will deny it?

Because it is the way humans have evolved. It's mostly unconscious, but snap judgments of other humans based solely on physical characteristics and facial expressions evolved as a way for humans to quickly assess threats and opportunities and determine relative social status of a new person to know how to interact with them. A deep discussion of this topic is far beyond the scope of this piece, but basically, it evolved because it worked. There is a ton of research and science on this, and most of it falls under what is called "signaling theory."

Because everyone is like this (and most of don't even realize it), you need to really pay attention to your author photo, and make sure you do it right. In this piece, I'm going to walk you through exactly how to do that.

Then we'll go through some examples of author photos, both good and bad, so can see what this looks like in practice.

THE AUTHOR PHOTO RULE THAT RULES THEM ALL

Here's the thing that makes author photos so hard to give advice about:

There is **not** one "right" way to do it. The "right" way all depends on what you're trying to achieve. But there is one overarching rule that you need to sear into your brain when it comes to author photos (or any profile photo):

Know what you want to signal to what audience, and then signal it properly.

This is the key to everything. The author photo for a CEO of a Fortune 500 company should be totally different from the author photo for an up-and-coming comedian. Why? Because they are signaling different things to different groups.

Generally speaking, the CEO's author photo should signal professionalism, effectiveness, reliability, and trust. The comedian's photo could be wacky, pensive, goofy, or even serious, all depending on his comedic style and what he/she wanted to signal.

To make sure you're taking the right author (or profile) photo, you need to ask yourself two questions:

1. What am I trying to say with my picture?

You say just as much with your appearance as you do with your words. Clearly words are more important in a book, but people judge books and judge the author (you) by what you look like.

The good news is that, within reason, it's much easier to construct the image you want in a still photo. You can emphasize whatever traits or aspect of your appearance you want, and you can also minimize any physical limitations that would be difficult to minimize in person; height, for example.

You can look serious or silly, professional or pretentious, positive or pessimistic, it's really up to you. But you cannot have them all at once.

You must make specific decisions about what you want to signal to the world through that picture. Decide that to yourself consciously, because once you do that, you'll be able to know the basic things that should and should not be in your picture.

2. Who am I trying to say it to?

It's not just what you are saying, it's also who you want to say it to that determines your author photo.

Why is that?

Because so much of signaling is about telling a specific group of people that you are one of them, or you are a type that they know. This means you must know the basic mindset and associations of that group, so you can make sure they see what you are trying to say.

For example, if you are trying to signal to corporations that you are a competent and reliable professional that they should trust and listen to, then you must understand that they see the conventional Western suit as a key signal not just of competence, but as a signal of membership in their tribe. Suits tell them that *you are one of them*. The best examples below are Patrick Lencioni and Jay Papasan.

Whereas, if you want to signal to the tech and start-up community, then wearing a suit sends the opposite signal; they see suits as a sign of being out of touch in their community. If you want them to see you as competent and tech minded, you want a picture like Eric Ries. He's telling them that he is one of them.

The importance of understanding this cannot be overstated. Remember, signaling is not just about what you are signaling, it's also about what other people are seeing, and what other people see depends almost entirely on what group they are part of and identify with.

Having a cutting-edge look in one field means you will be excluded in others, so knowing who you are trying to signal to and what signals they respond to is key for you.

This is all abstract. We'll show several examples of author photos, both good and bad, and break them down for you:

Joanna Penn

This is a classic author photo. This sig-
nals warmth and openness. Joanna has
a broad, authentic smile in her face; you
can almost see her enthusiasm and joy.

By making the photo black and white, and
cropped closely to her head, she focuses
you on the things she wants you to know
about her—she's positive, optimistic, and encouraging.

This makes sense; Joanna writes a lot of books for authors about writing, publishing, and marketing. She is a teacher, and this photo signals both trust and warmth.

Lisa Cartwright

This is not a good author photo at all.
First of all, it's tilted to the side in a
weird angle. Second, it's poorly color
corrected with poor resolution, and
dark. Third, the smile seems forced
and awkward.

These are all poor signals. Your first unconscious thought is something along the lines of, "Why is it not centered?" This picture signals unprofessionalism, amateurishness, and lack of emotional connection.

Michael Lewis

This picture could be in the dictionary for "classic high-status male author photo." He is smiling authentically with his eyes and has a head tilt, which signals both warmth and interest. His arms are casually crossed and his shirt is unbuttoned, which signals casualness and comfort. He has a tasteful button  down shirt, worn casually, and his hair is cut in a modern style, which all signal professionalism, but also comfort.

This picture tells a very clear story: this is a person who has done a lot in his life and is very comfortable with himself and his work.

Giff Constable

This is not good at all. He has a parted, flat hair style, his smile is toothy and goofy, and his shirt is distracting and visually unappealing. He's frail and has a thin neck and is slightly hunched over in a way that accentuates that aspect. The background of the photo is pure white, giving a jarring feel to his appearance, as if he is coming out of the screen.

Understand that I am NOT making fun of how he was born. Everything I commented on (and most of the things that people judge you on) are *things he can control*. He can control his hairstyle, his shirt, his posture, his smile, and the background of the photo.

This pictures sends several negative signals, the main one being that he has no aesthetic or professional taste. The fact that he did not take any time or spend any energy on his appearance at all, or if he did, he is so socially unskilled that he did this bad of a job, is generally a very negative signal.

But—not always. If he is writing a book for specific tribe that approves of these signals—in this case "nerdy" engineers—and he wants to signal to them that he are part of their tribe, this author photo actually does that. If that is the only audience we wants to talk to, then this photo actually accomplishes that.

The problem is that is it repels anyone that does not identify directly with that audience (which is most people).

Eric Ries

Compare this photo to the one above; it's the complete opposite. Physically, Eric and Giff are very similar. But the photos feel totally different, don't they?

Look at the signals: Eric has a simple hairstyle, his glasses are contemporary, his smile is authentic (but not toothy and goofy), and he's not slumping or accentuating any negative physical aspects of his appearance. His shirt is stylish without being ostentatious, and perhaps most important, look at the background. It is bottom lit and color shifting, which gives it a modern feel that is reminiscent of technology and the future.

Eric's audience is the same basic one as Giff's, but Eric's photo sends totally different signals. Eric is still appealing to a serious technical audience, but he is not turning off a mainstream audience. In fact, this photo displays a very sophisticated understanding of how he is trying to position himself: a serious technical insider, but not a socially awkward nerd.

Patrick Lencioni

This is a very traditional business professional author photo. Everything about this photo says that this man is an American business executive: solid, stable, trustworthy, and part of the establishment.

The suit is tailored, dark, expensive, and tasteful, and he has a tie on. His wedding ring is clearly showing. His hair is graying, combed but not stiff, and his smile is there, but not too excited or awkward. He is sitting in front of whiteboard, a signal for teaching and presentations (which is high status in the corporate world).

This makes sense. Patrick's entire market is traditional corporate America, and this picture speaks directly to them, telling them that even though he has some new ideas (the whiteboard), he is still one of them.

Jay Papasan

Jay has a different version of the business professional author photo. He is signaling that he's a legitimate businessman, but younger and more modern and hip.

He is wearing a suit that is dark and tasteful, but he has no tie, and his top button is undone. The background is green and environmental, another code for openness and modernity.

Andrii Sedniev

There are a lot of problems here. Start with the tie; it has poorly matched colors, it's off center, and it's clearly cheap. Then look at the shirt. The collar is not even tucked into his jacket. The tailoring of both jacket and shirt are clearly off the rack, and furthermore, the material for both shirt and jacket appear to be shiny, which is generally a signal for cheap in suits.

His haircut is a slightly grown-out buzz cut, which not only signals youth and inexperience, it also signals sloppiness. He didn't even bother to get his hair cut for his professional photo.

His smile is forced and uncomfortable, as if he is unsure of himself. Everything about this photo says "amateur." Just by looking at the photos, you can tell that Patrick and Jay are serious, established professionals, and that Andrii is not.

This is an example of a great author photo (for men or women). Look at the signals, all saying the same basic things, telling a coherent story about her taste, her warmth, and her ability:

1. She is sitting in a very design-forward chair, and this signals great aesthetic taste.

2. The shot is in an empty warehouse-style loft, which signals a specific design sensibility, one that is contemporary and minimalist.

3. It's aligned down a corridor, with pillars showing in the background in a symmetrical way, while she is slightly off center, giving her the perspective. This signals a deep understanding of design principles.

4. She is dressed in a classic and perfectly tailored outfit, with very stylish leather boots. This signals both excellent personal taste and business conservatism all at once.

5. She's looking away from the camera and smiling warmly, as if she's casually talking to someone in the background, signaling warmth and approachability.

6. She's very pretty, which this photo both hides and accentuates. She hides it by dressing in a traditionally male outfit (button-down shirt and black pants), but she accentuates

it by tailoring the outfit to make it feminine and leaving an extra button open.

7. The photo is black and white, which signals functionality and classic sense.

Just think about how this photo makes you feel. You're attracted to her and drawn in by her warmth and smile (but not in a sexual way). You know she's fashionable and has great aesthetics, and you can see her design style. But the picture is not of a self-indulgent fashion dilettante, so you take her seriously as an intelligent, professional CEO.

Photos are much harder for serious female CEOs than they are for men (for many reasons), and Mona walked that line perfectly (disclosure: Mona is a client of Book In A Box).

Harshajyoti Das

This is not an example of a bad author photo per se, but rather a very bad decision.

This first problem is that there are two people in the photo. Unless the book is authored by both of them, this is the first bad decision.

This picture signals a specific set of topics. If the author were writing books about kayaking, or water sports, or adventure, or anything related to the picture, this might be a good picture.

Unfortunately, this is an unknown author who writes generic marketing books. What is someone looking for credibility and authority in marketing going to think when they see this picture? That they should trust this author's skills...because he kayaks?

Finally, the sunglasses...Really? It's not even bright out.

Johnny Truant

This is another example of a very specific decision, except this is probably a good one. Through the look—eating the apple, and the unkempt but still fashionable clothes—this author photo signals that the author fits the model of a slightly naughty bad boy writer.

Since this author, Johnny Truant, writes funny serial fiction (one series is called *Fat Vampire*), this is a great decision. His material is edgy, tongue in cheek, and fun, and his author photo tells his audience, "I'm the type of person who would write that type of book."

Consistent in signals and material, and thus a good decision. Whereas, if Johnny were writing a book on nursing home consulting, this would be a bad set of signals to send.

TWO PICTURES OF THE SAME AUTHOR

Patrick Vlaskovits

Bad   **Good**

In this case, the author has two different photos. The first is too dark, there is no smile, and it is poorly cropped. In the second, it is well cropped, he has a good smile, and he is dressed in professional but casual clothes.

Like we said before, part of the "bad" versus "good" decision is about what signals you are trying to send to whom. If Patrick were an essayist and social commentator, perhaps the first photo would work. That picture signals intellectualism, self-seriousness, and pensive thought.

But that's not what his books are about, nor the audience he is trying to signal to. His books are about entrepreneurship, branding, and start-ups. To speak to that audience, you are better off being optimistic, positive, and warm—which the second picture signals.

James Altucher

Bad   Good

This is not so much a case of different pictures being good for different purposes, but a case of one picture being objectively worse than the other.

The first picture makes James look a disjointed crazy person. His glasses are off center, his hair is disheveled, he is a ratty white T-shirt, and the picture appears to be a random candid. James was actually using this as his author photo when he came to us.

I immediately asked his wife to take a picture that was professional looking but still reflected the quirkiness and weird genius that people love about him. She took the second picture, which is wonderful. He's dressed in dark and fashionable clothes and is set against a pleasant background, all of which signal competence and professionalism.

But he's also signaling quirkiness and humor: sitting cross-legged, retaining his trademark curly fro, and with a mischievous smile. It reflects who James is, while still signaling that he's serious and professional and has taste.

(Disclosure: James has been a client of Lioncrest Publishing, which is a division of Book In A Box.)

HOW TO TAKE YOUR AUTHOR PHOTO

Unless you are a very good photographer, I HIGHLY recommend you go to a photography studio and get your photo professionally done. There is no substitute for the skills of a professional photographer.

And as an added benefit, they will tend to be honest with you and make sure your photo sends the signals you want it to send, whereas you or a friend might fool yourself.

Some places to hire a pro:

Model Mayhem [Free to $500+][17]

Obviously, a database of models is a magnet for photographers, and Model Mayhem has a directory specifically for finding photographers.

The best part: There's a Time-for-Print option where newer photographers will photograph you for free. If you want to learn more about that option, read this article on How to Get Professional Portraits Taken For Free.[18]

---

17   http://www.modelmayhem.com/

18   http://mochagirlspitstop.wordpress.com/2012/07/16/how-to-get-professional-portraits-taken-for-free/

GigSalad [Prices Vary][19]

GigSalad is like Craigslist for booking services for events or productions. If you search "Headshot Photography," you'll get a list of dozens of photographers in your city who specialize in the exact kind of pictures you need.

HOW TO TAKE A PHOTO YOURSELF

If you can't or won't hire a good photographer, then you'll have to do this yourself. That's not impossible, but it can be a pain. I know it seems easy and obvious to do a good photo, but getting it right is actually much harder than you realize. If you insist on doing this yourself, we recommend learning a few things about lighting and photography first.

How to Take Professional Headshot with an iPhone[20]

Although we don't necessarily recommend using an iPhone, this is the best article on the Internet explaining everything you need to know to take a pro headshot, including lighting, equipment, common problems, locations, and editing.

Digital Photography School[21]

Tons more information than you could possibly consume on photography, portraits, and cameras. If you want to dive deeper into any part of the process, this is a good place to start, specifically their article on How to Take the Perfect Headshot.[22]

---

19   https://www.gigsalad.com/

20   http://www.sitebuilderreport.com/blog/how-to-take-your-own-professional-headshot-with-an-iphone

21   http://digital-photography-school.com/tips

22   http://digital-photography-school.com/how-to-take-the-perfect-headshot-six-tips/

TESTING YOUR AUTHOR PHOTO

If you are unsure whether or not your author photo is conveying the signals you want there is a way to test this: use a service called PhotoFeeler.[23] You can upload your photo, and get ratings on multiple dimensions that tell you exactly what people think about it. We've just started testing it and it works great so far.

READY TO MOVE ON?

→ Decide what attributes you want your author photo to convey

→ Take a professional author photo

→ If you'd like, test your photo on PhotoFeeler to see if it signals the correct attributes

---

Once your author photo is taken, it's time for the last stage of the pre-publishing process: registering your ISBN number.

---

23 https://www.photofeeler.com/

UNDERSTAND ISBNS

ISBNs (or International Standard Book Numbers) are 10- to 13-digit numbers created for the express purpose of intimidating authors and making them feel like the publishing process is more complicated than it is.

We're kidding. Sort of.

ISBNs can feel confusing to new authors, but only because they aren't well explained. Basically, the purpose of the ISBN is to allow bookstores and publishers to identify the book. When there are two books with the same title, the ISBN makes it clear that they're different books. When the title of a book is misprinted, the ISBN makes it clear that it's not a different book.

Where things get shady is the pricing. Bowker charges $129 for an ISBN, so people seem to naturally think there must be much more to it than a few digits. *Where's the system? There must be something I'm missing!*

There isn't. It is literally just a number used by the industry to track book identity.

You'll write the number inside your book and on the back cover, you'll plug it in when you load the book up on Amazon, and it'll remain in Bowker's database to identify the books they're registered. That's it.

DO I NEED AN ISBN?

Although we tried to make this book as linear as possible in your decisions, there are a few places in the process where you'll likely need to loop back around. This is one of them. Whether or not you need to purchase an ISBN depends on the printer you're using for the book.

You can come back once you've made the decision, but the basic idea is this:

If you are publishing the book through CreateSpace, and only intend to sell it on Amazon, CreateSpace will provide the ISBN for free. This is the path we'd recommend to most authors, but it'll depend on your goals for the book (we'll discuss the details of this decision in Chapter 20).

If you are publishing the book through any other printer, you'll need to buy your own ISBN.

Like we mentioned above, buying your own ISBN is unreasonably expensive. They cost $129 apiece and you need a separate ISBN for each version of your book (paperback, ebook, audiobook, etc.).

One positive is that there are pretty substantial volume discounts. Buying one ISBN is $129, but buying ten is only $295, and 100 is $575. This leads a lot of people to decide to split a larger order with a fellow author.

Splitting a bulk purchase is a great idea, just be careful: The ISBNs will need to be purchased under one imprint (which is the name that will show up as the publisher on sites like Amazon).

It's not a problem, you can create sub-imprints through Bowker that solves the problem, just be prepared for a little bit of a headache in dealing with it if you decide to go this route.

HOW DO I BUY AN ISBN?

As we discussed Part 2, if you're working with CreateSpace and want to publish the book only through Amazon, there's no need to purchase an additional ISBN.

If you're going through another platform, or want to be able to publish the book elsewhere, you'll need to buy an ISBN.

Go to http://myidentifier.com and buy the ISBN. This is Bowker's website (the company that issues the ISBNs) and is the most trustworthy option. Anything you find in a Google search is likely a reseller and can be a lot less reliable.

At this point, you should have the manuscript finished and locked in. You should have the title, description, the author bio, picture, and an ISBN. You are now ready to start with the design and creation of the finished book files for you to publish.

Congratulations! You now have all the assets you need to start the publishing process. Now, it's time to turn your attention to designing your book.

GET THE RIGHT BOOK COVER

We could write an entire book just on book covers. It's a deeply interesting subject with a wealth of both art and data behind it...but we won't do that to you, because you probably don't care.

Instead, we're going to make this as simple as possible for you to get your book cover right.

This chapter will walk you through what you need to know about book covers, why you need a book cover designer, how to find a good one, how to work with them to ensure they create the cover you want, and how to make sure you have the right cover when the process is done.

1. Your Book Will Be Judged by its Cover (and This Is Good)

This is a fact:

Everyone judges books by their covers.

If you are silently complaining about this, stop. The best thing to do is accept it, and then focus on making sure you have the best book cover possible, one that draws attention and entices readers.

(**Note:** If you're honest with yourself, you probably judge books by their cover as well, so your complaining is not only ineffective, it's hypocritical.)

Not only does it not help to complain about this fact, you are missing that *it's good news that people judge your book by the cover.* Otherwise, they might not make any judgment at all, and no judgment means they aren't buying or reading it.

This is the thing that authors who don't pay attention to the book cover don't understand: It doesn't matter how great your book is, because if the cover repels your audience they will never give it a chance.

The entire point of the cover, in fact, is to ***help your audience realize that they should be reading your book.***

You should look at the cover as a chance to win a reader, as a way to reach someone who needs to read your book. And if you don't do this, then your book cover will not be very good, and will not attract the readers you want to your book.

2. You Should NOT Design Your Own Book Cover

When you want a bottle of beer, do you brew it yourself?

When you want a new coat, do you sew it yourself?

When you need a new bar of soap, do you make it yourself?

No. You buy all of those things from people who are experts at making them.

Book covers are no different. You should have your book cover designed by a professional to get a professional cover.

It's the same reason why most people don't make homebrewed beer even though it's not terribly complicated, and why no one wears homemade clothes, even though they're easy to make—they suck in comparison to the professional alternatives.

The only real difference between beer and coats and book covers is that some people *think* they can design their own book covers, even if they really can't.

Don't do it. It will suck. Get a professional.

3. There Are Objectively Good and Bad Book Covers

Please don't be the person who thinks that because some art is subjective, then everything related to art—like book covers—is subjective.

No. That is wrong.

A book cover is a piece of art, yes, but it is a piece of art with a specific purpose, and all book covers can be measured against this specific statement:

Book covers exist to give visual form to written content.

A great cover makes someone in your intended audience say "I need to read that," by *showing* them why the book matters to them in a way they can immediately grasp (or at least raising their interest enough to want to learn more).

Another way to think about it is framed by Chip Kidd, a famous book cover designer, who said that "a book cover is a distillation of the content, almost like what your book would look like as a haiku."

That being said, a good book cover is not just an expression of the idea behind a book, it's the way that the audience first engages that idea. It's marketing. And that is how you measure an objectively good book cover:

A good book cover matters to the author (because it shows what's in the book) and the audience (because it makes them interested in what is in the book).

WHAT DO YOU DO BEFORE YOU HIRE A BOOK COVER DESIGNER?

Now you understand what purpose a cover serves and why a professional book cover is important, you're ready to find a good book cover designer and hire them, right?

Not so fast.

The main problem any book designer will tell you is that the author gives them no idea what they want, or vague and ambiguous cover ideas, and the two never get on the same page.

You can avoid this problem by doing some work prior to finding a book cover designer. Not only will this get you a better cover, it can save you a lot of money.

1. Look at lots of book covers, both in your field and out

The first thing you need to do is get an idea of what other books in your field are like, and maybe to get some ideas from them.

Something that is less obvious but also important is looking at books in lots of other fields to get ideas as well. Just because your book is about psychology doesn't mean you have to use the same tropes as all psychology books; you can use some ideas from business or self-help books, or even novels.

Once you spend some time looking at a lot of book covers in your genre, you'll be shocked at how repetitive they are. That's common. Don't feel bad about using some of these tropes—they exist for a reason, and they will help you, actually. It is a good thing for people to be able to identify your book as being in the genre you want to be in.

Also, don't feel bad about taking inspiration from your favorite books. Everything is derivative to some extent—just don't flat out copy.

2. Pick several that are close to what you want

As you look at them, start to save a few examples of the ones you really like, or ones that have elements that you really like. The reason you're doing this should be obvious: you need to *show* your designer what you like (not just try to describe it).

Scour the Internet and bookstores for covers that capture the aesthetic you're going for, and save pictures of all of them. Designers see the world visually, and the best way to get a point across to them is to show them.

At Book In A Box, we have a document with 10 very different covers that we walk authors through to get a sense for their taste. You can download it for your own use here.[24]

3. Pick a few brands or other pieces of art that capture your aesthetic

This might sound a bit pretentious, but it's actually useful: don't just limit yourself to book covers. Pull in logos, websites, art, photos, or pretty much any image you can find that is some way is something like what you want on your book cover.

This is essentially creating a collage (some people call this a mood board) of visual inspiration and ideas that can help your designer understand how to best get your book's message across to your audience.

---

24 http://bookinabox.com/resources

4. Hand draw a couple quick mock-ups yourself

This isn't totally necessary, but for some people, it can really help them. If you have a very specific vision for your book cover, what we recommend is actually hand drawing a mock-up of the cover.

Of course it will be bad. That's fine; believe it or not, a really bad mock-up is still much better than anything you can describe with words.

In short, this is because using words to describe images is always problematic, so the more you can give a visual description to the designer, the better. Even if your mockups are terrible drawings that you put on a napkin, they will help your designer turn them into something really good.

Furthermore, doing a mock-up enables you to see quickly see if an idea is working or not. As the author Charlie Hoehn says,

"I can't emphasize how important it is to come up with a concept first and to do the mock-ups yourself. Every author I know is inevitably disappointed with the cover concepts their publisher or designer comes up with. But the truth is that no one understands the spirit and meaning of the book better than the person who wrote it. All authors should try to envision the exact cover they want, then draw it out on paper."

HOW DO YOU FIND A BOOK COVER DESIGNER?

There are a TON of options. We're going to break down the basic categories here, tell you about the major places, and what we think of them:

1. DIY ($0)

We would NOT recommend this—as we've said repeatedly. But if your goal is to keep cost to zero, it's the only way to go.

We're not going to get into the technical aspects of book design in this book, but if you want your book to look professional, it's going to take a lot of learning and a lot of practice. Good designers spend YEARS training.

For DIY, your best bet is to use the Canva book cover tool (https://www.canva.com/create/book-covers/). You can use these to make the process easier, but don't expect to end up with a great result. All the professionals use Photoshop or Illustrator, but those are difficult tools you can't just waltz into and learn in a day.

2. Fiverr ($5–40)

Fiverr is a marketplace of services available for $5 or so. There are a ton of book cover designers on Fiverr, but almost all of them are absolute garbage.

We've never used Fiverr for cover design at Book In A Box, but friends of ours have been able to find a couple designers who are good. Typically they do a great job, get a ton of 5-star reviews, and then disappear to another site where they can charge more than $5 for their work. But, if you search diligently enough, there are gems out there.

Basically, think of it this way. If someone has any design talent, why would they work for $5 a cover? Maybe you hit the jackpot and find the rock star who hasn't been discovered yet, but more likely you're getting what you pay for.

3. Upwork ($50–200)

The next step up the quality ladder would be a freelance network like Upwork. Similar to Fiverr, the overall quality on Upwork is pretty low. Unlike Fiverr, there are more high quality designers hidden on there, because they're able to charge reasonable prices. Expect to take your time to find the right person on one of these sites, but you will be able to find them. Job ads typically get dozens if not hundreds of responses, and designers typically link a portfolio of past work.

Screen out anyone with negative reviews, and then focus 100% of your screening time on judging their portfolios. Portfolios are the only thing that gives you a real picture into the quality of their work. If you like their past work, you'll probably like their future work. Everything else is just marketing.

4. 99designs ($300–600)

99designs (and similar sites like Crowdspring) aren't necessarily a step up from Upwork quality, in fact, sometimes the designers are worse. But the model can often make it worthwhile.

How these sites work is that you post a detailed design brief to their site and pay a flat fee. Dozens of designers take your brief, design a cover, and post it for your approval. You then have the option to choose the winning designer to take the cover from, or, if you don't like any of the designs, get a full refund with no hassle.

99designs is great as a first option to test if a great cover would be worth the money to you. That way you can see the designs, get some ideas, and hopefully find a great cover. But, if not, no harm, and you can go back to the drawing board with the other options.

We'd recommend doing the Silver contest (which costs $499). The lower end contests really repel the better designers on the site, and the higher end ones don't seem to garner much higher quality (and actually tend to get fewer submissions).

5. Independent Designer ($500–$2000+)

The highest quality option is always to hire an independent contractor. A lot of the best book cover designers in the world, who work regularly with major publishing houses, are available to hire on a freelance basis, and their prices can be pretty reasonable. This is what we do for our clients at Book In A Box, and it's very worthwhile.

There are a few ways to find these people. One of the best options is Reedsy, a freelance marketplace designed specifically for authors. Reedsy screens the freelancers, only letting the best in. It's the highest quality marketplace of book designers we've found, and we highly recommend it.

The other option is to go to more general design sites, like Behance or Dribbble, and search for book designers there. They can be a bit slow to respond and difficult to get in touch with, but the quality there is outstanding as well.

IT'S NOT JUST A FRONT COVER!

In a world where some authors are only creating Kindle books, while others are creating paperbacks and hard-covers, the default scope of work for cover designers can become fuzzy. It's important to always be clear what exactly you're hiring the designer for before getting started.

- If you're only doing an ebook, you'll just need a front cover for Amazon.
- If you're also doing a paperback, you'll need a spine and back cover designed.
- If you're also doing a hardcover, you'll need a file for the case binding (the physical book) and a separate file for the jacket (the sleeve that goes over the book).

The assumption should be that these designs are included in a normal "cover design quote," but if not, you can expect to pay an additional 25-50% on top of the front cover price to get the rest of the design work done.

Always make sure to be clear on this before the designer gets started.

HOW DO YOU WORK WITH YOUR BOOK COVER DESIGNER?

Once you have established contact and negotiated price, then comes discussion of your cover idea. Here is where all that work you did before comes into play.

First off, if possible, get on the phone. Email is very hard to effectively communicate with strangers, especially about abstract concepts like design.

Prior to the call, send them a brief. This should include all the book covers you like, all the logos and other pictures you like, and everything else you assembled. If you created one, also send them your mock-up of the cover. Do this at least a day ahead of time; designers tend to like to have time to digest images and ideas.

Once on the call, walk them through your thinking: What do you like about each cover? What do you dislike? What do you want your cover to feel like? What emotions do you want it to elicit in the reader? What signals are you trying to send, and to what audience? How does your mock-up or cover idea convey this?

The more you explain all of your thinking to the cover designer, the better they will do.

Ask them for at least three mock-ups, one that is derived from your idea, and two that are their own ideas.

Once you get the mock-ups back, if one jumps out at you, great. Give specific notes and feedback to get it where you want, and then you're done, great.

If you aren't happy with any of the covers, that's okay too. Get back on the phone with the designer, and—while being polite—be as specific as possible about what you would like different.

This is not about getting angry or frustrated with the cover designer. They aren't in your head, and if their mock-ups did not fit your vision, that's okay. Just be clearer and more methodical in your description, and you'll get there.

Remember this: Your cover designer is a human who has feelings, but also a professional who wants to do a great job. You are both on the same team. You can be firm, but also polite and understanding.

If you are unsure about how to evaluate your cover, the next section explains.

HOW CAN YOU CHECK IF YOU HAVE A GOOD BOOK COVER?

Once you have a cover, or you think you have one, here is how you check to see if it's right:

1. Does it stand out?

This is crucial. Look at it from all angles; print it out and put it across the room. Think of every possible way someone will look at it—on a screen, in a bookstore, etc.—and make sure it stands out that way. Can you read the title? Is the image clear?

Check it as a thumbnail too. Does your cover look good when you shrink it down to a tiny thumbnail? That's how most of your readers will see it, as a small image on Amazon.

You could think of your book cover like a billboard, trying to catch the attention of browsers as they speed by. Billboards usually have six words or less. You have to "get it" at 60 miles per hour, in 3 to 5 seconds.

2. Does it have a clear focus?

Establish a principal focus for the cover—nothing is more important than this one thing. Your book is about something, and the cover ought to reflect that one idea clearly. You must have one element that takes control, that commands the overwhelming majority of attention, of space, of emphasis on the cover.

Don't fall into the trap of loading up your cover with too many elements, three or four photos, illustrations, maps, "floating" ticket stubs. This just confuses people, and confused people become repelled.

3. Does it say what the book is and who the book is for?

Not only does your book stand out, but at a glance your audience ought to know:

- The genre of your book
- The general subject matter or focus, and
- Some idea of the tone or position of the book

A truly great book is one that captures the book inside in some fundamental and perhaps unforeseen way.

4. Did you explore enough options?

Maybe some people have "love at first sight" when it comes to cover designs. The artist creates one comp, the entire team falls in love with it, and the whole process takes 15 minutes. I guess that happens, but that's certainly not something I've experienced.

We've had authors who went through more than 25 different designs. I'm not talking about 25 rough sketches or napkin concepts. I'm talking about 25 deliberate, hard fought comps. That is rare, but it happens.

The challenge is that as an author, toward the end of the process, there's a part of you that wants it to be done. It's very tempting to pick a design you kind of like just to get the whole thing finished.

Fight that with everything you've got. You need to find something you love, not just like. You didn't half-write the book, don't half-design the cover.

5. Did you make the brave choice?

We see this happen all the time: we'll give an author three mock-ups, and there will almost always be a bad choice, a solid choice, and a great choice.

The great choice will almost always require the author to be brave in selecting it. It will have some angle or position that is novel in your field, or make a statement that is controversial, or just be different in a way that will make you just a little uncomfortable.

I'd say that only about 25% of authors pick the brave choice, and it saddens me every time.

You don't have to make the brave choice, but it's almost always the best one (if there is a brave choice available, this isn't always true). Be aware if this happens to you.

The solid choice is not bad, but it means your book won't stand out or get the attention it deserves. The brave choice means it will.

It you are unsure how to define brave, here is a way to think about it:

The brave choice says what everyone is thinking, but not saying out loud.

READY TO MOVE ON?

→ Put together your book design brief

→ Find and hire a book cover designer

→ Work with your book cover designer to create a great cover

→ Confirm that it accomplishes your goals and meets the criteria above

Once your front cover is designed, you are ready to pause the front cover design to create the book's interior print layout.

DESIGN YOUR BOOK'S INTERIOR

(**Note:** This chapter is about designing the interior of your print book. If you want to publish your book in ebook format ONLY—which means no paperback or hardcover—you can skip this chapter entirely.)

Have you ever started to read a book, and on the first page—before you've engaged the actual content—you immediately get a bad feeling and can't take the book seriously? And sometimes you can't even explain why?

This is the impact of interior design. Interior design is one of those things that you never notice...unless it's wrong.

Despite how simple it seems (or perhaps because of it), interior layout is one of the major factors that separates amateurish books from professional ones.

How complicated can the inside layout of a book be? We're about to find out.

BEFORE YOU START INTERIOR LAYOUT

Before you even start the interior layout discussion, you need to decide on the size of your book. Changing trim sizes down the road can be a big hassle, so it's worth getting this figured out first before any work is done.

There aren't any hard and fast rules around trim size, but there are general trends. Trim sizes are always measured in inches, with the horizontal measurement first, then the vertical.

The most common book size is 6 × 9. It works for books of any style and is generally the industry standard.

At Book In A Box, we tend to use 5.5 × 8.5. This slightly smaller size tends to be more common with business books. There are a lot of books that are 5 × 8 as well, but I'd consider that the lower limit before the book starts looking awkwardly small.

The following page lists the trim sizes that CreateSpace offers as "conventional" book sizes.

WHY IS INTERIOR LAYOUT SO COMPLICATED?

Interior layout is easy to dismiss. It's just formatting words on a page. Google Docs does that automatically. What's the big deal?

Trim Size	Color Interior Maximum Page Count	Black & White Interior Maximum Page Count	
	White Paper	White Paper	Cream Paper
5" x 8"	480	828	740
5.06" x 7.81"	480	828	740
5.25" x 8"	480	828	740
5.5" x 8.5"	480	828	740
6" x 9"	480	828	740
6.14" x 9.21"	480	828	740
6.69" x 9.61"	480	828	740
7" x 10"	480	828	740
7.44" x 9.69"	480	828	740
7.5" x 9.25"	480	828	740
8" x 10"	480	440	400
8.25" x 6"	212	220	200
8.25" x 8.25"	212	220	200

The first thing to realize is that there's a lot more that goes into designing the interior of a book than you might expect. These are just some of the decisions that must be made:

+ Trim size (as explained above)
+ Color vs. black and white
+ Other physical considerations (paperback vs. hardcover, paper stock, etc.)
+ Font selection
+ Spacing decisions
+ Design elements in the header
+ Sidebars (if any)
+ If/how you want to incorporate illustrations, photography, or other graphics

There are also all the more nerdy publishing details that your proofreader should have caught but likely didn't, like making sure you're using the right dashes in the right places (hyphens and em and en dashes all have distinct uses). The same goes for quotation marks (straight vs. curly vs. foot/inch marks—all different things), mathematical symbols (× vs. x), and nearly every other symbol you can (but won't) think of.

And, because it's a book and you don't want anything slipping through, it's also crucial that it's manually checked for widows and orphans (the single line at end of a paragraph that ends up at the top of the next page, or a single word on a line by itself), or any other formatting that can come across as unprofessional or ugly.

But, truthfully, that's only a small part of the problem. The main reason that it's so complicated and expensive is that *nobody wants to do it.*

Interior layout is hard, tiring work, and requires a lot of hours from someone with at least a strong baseline of design skills. Most designers went into the field because they love working on beautiful, creative projects. Interior print layout has those elements, sure—but also demands a lot of precision and "boring" practical considerations that designers don't always like to be constrained by (not unlike, say, industrial design).

So who *does* offer high quality interior layout? There are some people who just love the detail of things like typography and layout. But most of them are not like that. Many are the type that have decided they're okay with using their talent working on comparatively plain pages that don't feel so creative, as long as they get paid extremely well for it.

Which leads us to a divide. The interior layout world is fundamentally split in half. Some of the options are extremely cheap ($100-200). These are the people you can find on sites like Upwork, or that you get through CreateSpace if you have them do your design. Frankly, they won't do a very good job.

The other half are expensive, usually $1500-2000+. These are the people who would rather be doing other things, so they charge high rates to make it worthwhile.

There is one other option, which we'll get to later in the chapter. We just wanted to paint the picture and provide the logic before explaining the options, as the huge discrepancy in prices can be a bit jarring if you don't understand it.

WHAT SHOULD A GOOD INTERIOR LAYOUT LOOK LIKE?

This is not an easy question to answer. Like we said earlier, very few people notice the interior layout—unless it's wrong, then it is a huge problem.

Here are the major elements of interior design. We are listing them, not because we expect you to learn them. We are listing them for two reasons:

1. So when you hire a professional interior designer to lay out your book for you (which we highly recommend), you have a list of things you can discuss with them.

2. So can know what good versus bad looks like.

BAD DESIGN

HERE IS AN EXAMPLE of **bad** page design. Painful right? You probably don't even want to read it. Power through it for a moment and right off the bat you'll notice a few things:

BAD TYPOGRAPHY

-**Poor font choices** (Cambria and Arial). Cambria (one of Word's default fonts) actually isn't that bad for the screen, but suffers in print. Arial is ubiquitous because it was a system font in Windows for so long, but is effectively just worse Helvetica.

-**Sloppy hyphenation/justification.** Professional layout software like Adobe InDesign uses powerful, customizable algorithms to help produce a natural text flow. Others, not so much.

-**The little things.** ALL CAPS, underlined text, "dumb quotes" and double dashes--there are hundreds of nuances that add up to text looking either professional, or like it came straight out of Word (and in this case it did--that's how this page was created).

BAD USE OF SPACE

Pretty much everywhere--the margins are too small, the space between lines is too tight, and space after each sentence is too big. It's a subtle thing but makes a huge difference in readability.

BAD STRUCTURE

Most writing apps include a defined hierarchy for organizing information--**Heading 1, Heading 2**, etc.--and most writers completely ignore it right out of the gate. Instead they opt for arbitrary or inconsistent headings that make it difficult for the reader to skim text quickly or understand how it is prioritized ("is this a new topic, or just a subsection?"). For example, although the three headings on this page all reference the same "level" of information, they are each styled differently.

HERE IS AN EXAMPLE of *good* page design. Right off the bat you'll notice some important differences:

GOOD TYPOGRAPHY

- *Professional Typefaces* (Adobe Caslon Pro and Brandon Text)
  Caslon is considered a very "safe" pick and a popular choice among book designers for good reason: it reads very comfortably and suits a wide variety of content.

- *Natural-looking Justification & Careful Hyphenation*
  There aren't any huge gaps between words or "ladders" of hyphens running down the side of a paragraph.

- *The Little Things Make a Big Difference*
  SMALL CAPS, "curly quotes," em dashes—and no underlines. That last one is news to most people, but apart from links, underlining is mostly a relic of the manual typewriter. Today we can show **emphasis** in *better*, more PROFESSIONAL ways.

GOOD USE OF SPACE

The text on this page has room to breathe, is set on a baseline grid, and has single spaces after punctuation (double-spacing is wrong, forget what your English teacher said). Nice, isn't it?

GOOD STRUCTURE

The information is clearly and consistently organized. Much easier for the reader to follow, absorb, reference and skim.

SHOULD I SKIP A PRINT VERSION ENTIRELY?

As you've seen already in this chapter, print books are a lot of work. So why should you even do them?

The reason is actually that you should do them precisely *because* they're a lot of work. The book market is flooded with thousands of new authors every day. As you know, it can be difficult to stand out.

Because of how challenging doing a good print book is, and how embarrassingly ugly it can be when done wrong, a lot of new authors are veering away from the challenge and publishing in ebook format only. In many circles, this has started to be a dividing line between books that should be taken seriously, and books that shouldn't. Many people see ebooks as "not real books" and dismiss them as less impressive than paperbacks.

We tend to disagree with this, but that doesn't mean we should ignore it. Creating a high quality paperback or hardcover version is one of the most powerful ways to make sure your book is taken seriously and seen as a "real" book. We wouldn't skip this step if credibility is a key goal of yours.

HOW TO DO INTERIOR PRINT LAYOUT

Like most steps in this process, you have two options: you can do it yourself, or you can hire someone more talented than you who does it professionally.

DIY

As we've already discussed, doing a cheap interior can completely change the perception of your book. But, if it's the only option that works for you financially, there are some ways to do it yourself. The easiest one is to use a template. You can download templates at bookinabox.com/resources. But those are for Microsoft Word. If you *really* want to go all out, you need to learn Adobe InDesign (Hint: *Don't* do that, if you value your time at greater than $0).

Professionals

If you're going to hire a designer, there are basically three options:

1. **The Cheap Route:** There are two ways to find cheap interior layout designers. The first is directly through CreateSpace. We'll dig into the specific details in Chapter 20, but for many of you CreateSpace will be the best way to publish your book. While going through the publishing process, they give you the option to hire them for interior layout. They're not better or worse than the other options of a similar price, but they make things simple.

The other cheap route option is to use a freelance marketplace like Upwork. As we described earlier in the chapter, the quality of these designs is really low. It's easy to delude yourself when you're looking at a computer screen to think that the PDF looks good, but we've tested this path enough times to know better.

Only use one of these cheap options if you're okay with the

book not looking entirely professional. We'd honestly recommend doing the DIY template option as a better alternative to hiring this quality of designer—that's how bad it usually turns out.

2. The Expensive Route: The other alternative is to hire a real pro. More than any other part of the book creation process, except maybe editing, there's a huge gap between good interior layout designers and bad ones. If you hire a bad editor, they're worse than useless. If you hire a great editor, they can completely transform your book. Same goes with interior layout.

If you want to go down this route, we've checked out the work quality from a lot of the various options. The ones we'd most highly recommend are:

+ The Book Designers (~ $2000)[25]
+ 1106 Design (~ $1500)[26]

The problem with the companies in this space isn't their quality; the quality is good. The problem is the price and the turnaround time.

Because they're in an industry with so little competition, they're able to move slow and overcharge. But if you just care about someone doing a great job, these firms are excellent places to turn.

25 http://bookdesigners.com/

26 http://1106design.com

READY TO MOVE ON?

→ Choose your trim size

→ Hire an interior print designer

With the interior layout done, you're ready to pass the page count back to the cover designer so they can create the spine and back cover.

DESIGN YOUR SPINE AND BACK COVER

Now that the interior layout is finished, it's time to finalize the cover files and get your book ready for print.

CREATE THE BOOK COVER TEMPLATE

The task of creating the files for the physical book is very precise. It's important that all the dimensions are right, and the formulas to calculate them are much more complicated than the simple rules for creating a Kindle cover.

Fortunately, printers will often create cover file templates for designers to work from, to ensure that all the dimensions are right.

Throughout this book, the assumption is that you will be printing through CreateSpace. If that's the case, they have a handy tool that allows you to do this automatically. Go here [27]and plug in the trim size, number of pages, ISBN, and paper type (we recommend using white paper, as CreateSpace's cream is a little too yellow), and they'll automatically generate the template for your designer to work from.

ORGANIZE YOUR SPINE AND BACK COVER

The next decision you'll need to make is what goes where on the back cover and spine. This is one of those areas where authors can freak themselves out feeling like they need to conform to some mysterious unwritten rules.

Don't do this!

There are no hard and fast rules about what belongs where on the back cover, only rules of thumb.

Here are some general guidelines:

1. The spine should contain the book title and the author's name. If you have a publishing imprint for the book, you can also include that on the spine. If not, don't worry about it. No reader cares.

Some book spines will include a miniature version of the front cover or a symbol related to the ideas in the book. Again, this is by no means necessary, but can be a nice touch when done right.

---

27 https://www.createspace.com/Help/Book/Artwork.do

Note: If your book is under 100 pages, there likely won't be enough room on the spine to put readable text. One alternative here is to leave the spine completely blank, but the better option in our opinion is to try to get the book over 100 pages. You can do this by making the page size smaller, or by adding extra elements like an Acknowledgements section, a Dedication, or a workbook in the back.

2. The back cover of paperbacks almost always includes the book description as the central piece of the cover. Authors will include a testimonial or blurb for the book above the description, an author bio, and author photo below the description (or both, or neither). It's up to you—the author bio and photo can be inside as well. And you can always leave the photo out if you desire.

For hardcover books (which CreateSpace can't publish, but you may be interested in publishing through another printer), the usual format is to put only testimonials or blurbs on the back cover. The description then goes on the left (front) flap, and the author photo and bio go on the right (back) flap.

In any case, make sure you leave enough space so that the description is large enough to be read. Shoot for a maximum of 200 words on the back cover of the book, and ideally less if you can make it work.

PASS EVERYTHING BACK TO YOUR DESIGNER

Now it's time to pass all this information back to your designer to work on the final files. They'll need the cover template from the printer, the description and other copy for back cover, and the ISBN of the book.

You should use the same designer that you used for the front cover to do the spine and back, to ensure a consistent style. You should have negotiated on the price for the full cover, including spine and back, from the start, and that should be the assumption.

If you weren't able to have this discussion beforehand and the designer was paid only to do the front cover (for example, if you used 99designs), feel free to ballpark an additional 30-50% on top of what you paid for the front cover to design the spine and back.

Once the designer sends back the finished cover files and you're happy with everything, you're ready for the next phase. You have all the files for your print book finished and ready to go.

READY TO MOVE ON?

→ Send the cover designer the final template, book description, and any other back cover assets

→ Work with the cover designer to create the full book jacket

Once your full book cover is designed, you're ready to create the ebook.

FORMAT YOUR EBOOK

(**Note:** If you decided to hire a pro to do your interior layout, they'll often include the ebook conversion in the process. If that's the case, feel free to skip this chapter.)

Compared to the horror of designing your print interior, designing an ebook is actually pretty straightforward. Unlike the manual work and design aesthetic that need to go into a print book, creating ebooks is mostly coding work and a lot of it is automated. The cost is lower, and the results are more consistent.

HOW TO CREATE YOUR EBOOK

Like most steps in this process, you have two options: you can do it yourself, or you can hire someone.

We're just going to be blunt about this: *don't do it yourself.*

UNDERSTANDING EBOOK FILE FORMATS

There are two standard ebook file formats that you'll see. Epub files (book.epub) is the universal standard, and is used by Apple iBook, Nook, Kobo, and most other ebook retailers. These files are a little more customizable, have a little more flexibility for design, and are frankly just easier to use.

Mobi files (book.mobi) are for Amazon Kindle. Because Amazon is the big player in the space, they are able to set their own standards that are different from anyone else's. Mobi files can be a little more complicated to edit, but they're crucial, as Amazon will be where the vast majority of your books are sold.

There are programs like Vellum that you can use (or you can create the code directly), but it just isn't worth it. Unlike with print books, the cheap ebook designers do a better job than you will, so it's not worth messing with.

As with some of the other design elements, there are three places we'd turn for varying qualities of ebook.

1. **Fiverr ($5):** As we discussed, Fiverr is a marketplace of services that are all available for $5. Obviously, no matter what you're getting, it isn't going to be of the highest quality, but with ebooks, they're actually passable. I wouldn't recommend them to an author who's overly concerned

with looking professional, or for a book with a lot of hierarchy and headers (you should go through in Word and tag the headers properly in advance, because a Fiverr designer won't get them right), but for authors with a seriously tight budget, it's an option.

2. **Upwork ($50-150):** Similar to book covers, Upwork is a good middle option. You can find pretty cheap talent and, if you look hard enough, pretty high quality people. Especially for something like ebook design—which isn't overly complicated—finding someone with a lot of experience, great reviews, and some good examples of past work is usually enough to ensure success.

3. **Professionals ($200-500):** The final option is to work with a firm that's really professional. The challenge here is that a lot of the companies that look professional are really just fancy middlemen between you and cheaper, overseas labor. Don't mistake a high price tag for professionalism.

Some reputable companies that I've heard good things about: Convert-A-Book,[28] Innodata,[29] Formax,[30] and Lapiz.[31]

If you don't want to mess around or waste any time and you just want it done right without the back-and-forth, these are probably your best options.

28 http://convertabook.com/

29 http://ebook.innodata.com

30 http://www.formax.us/XML-Conversion.html

31 http://www.lapizdigital.com/Services/Conversion/Conversion.aspx

That means you have successfully created a finished book cover, print interior, and ebook file(s). Congratulations! The hardest part is over and you're almost there.

READY TO MOVE ON?

→ Decide which ebook file formats you need

→ Hire a professional to create your ebook

PUBLISH YOUR PRINT BOOK

Now that you have all the final files prepared for your book, the last step is to upload them and make the book available for sale. This chapter is going to cover how to do this for your print book, and the following chapter will run through the same thing for your ebook.

WHAT ARE THE DIFFERENT OPTIONS TO PRINT YOUR BOOK?

There are fundamentally two ways to print your book: **print on demand** or **commercial offset**.

Print on demand (POD) printers are just what they sound like. They take your files, get them all set up, but then print the books on an as-needed basis. If someone orders one copy on Amazon, they print one copy. If you want 500 copies for a conference, they print 500 copies. They price per copy doesn't change, and there are no minimum orders.

Commercial offset printing is the opposite. Commercial offset printers typically run large orders of books. The books are then warehoused and shipped out as they're needed. With commercial offset printers, the price per book drops dramatically as more copies are ordered.

With that understanding, there are four situations when commercial offset printing might make sense for you:

1. **You want a color interior for your book:** CreateSpace offers color interiors, but it makes the books preposterously expensive, usually $20+. At this price, you need to charge almost $35 on Amazon just to break even on the book. It's better to go elsewhere.

2. **You know you're going to want to order in large quantities:** CreateSpace is great because books are reasonably priced, down to the lowest quantities. The other side of this coin is that there are no price breaks at high quantities. If you're ordering 3000 books or more, there's likely a less expensive option.

3. **You need fancy design elements printed:** Printing features like spot lamination on the cover, one of those color inserts that has photos in the middle of the book, or any other creative design elements, can't be done by CreateSpace.

4. **You need a hardcover version:** For the time being,

CreateSpace doesn't offer hardcovers. There are other print on demand platforms that do (like Ingram Spark), but because of high cost and shaky integration with Amazon, we recommend going to a commercial offset printer if you want hardcovers produced.

We do not cover the details of commercial offset printing in this book, as the techniques and information needed vary greatly. If you decide to go this route, discuss the details with whichever printer you decide to use.

The rest of this chapter will focus on the authors who don't fit into the above four categories, for whom CreateSpace is the best choice.

WHAT IS CREATESPACE?

CreateSpace is a company that provides print on demand services and easy integration with Amazon. Why is it so easy? Because Amazon owns them.

CreateSpace couldn't be more simple. You upload your files, enter the relevant information, and in 1-5 days your paperback book will be live and available for sale on Amazon.

Depending on the length of your book, your cost per book will be in the $2.50–$4 range. You can order copies directly at this price, or sell them on Amazon and have the book cost taken directly off the top of people's purchase price.

CreateSpace also offers a few other options.

First off, you can upload your ebook through their platform. I wouldn't recommend it, as they take an additional percentage above KDP (which you'll learn about in the next chapter) and don't provide any extra value. Skip right past this option when they offer it.

Secondly, you can have CreateSpace help with the design of your book's cover and interior. Again, I wouldn't take them up on this option. It would be great if there was an all-in-one place that could really provide a great service, and they may get there one day, but for the time being, books designed by CreateSpace look amateur. Follow the process in this book and upload the designed interior files instead.

HOW DO YOU USE CREATESPACE?

CreateSpace is pretty intuitive, especially armed with the work you've done so far to be prepared without any problems. With that being said, there may still be times when you feel uncertain about what to do when uploading your book.

If that's the case, we created a video walkthrough that explains how to upload your book to CreateSpace, and explains each of the fields you'll need to fill out, and common mistakes to avoid.

Go to bookinabox.com/resources if you'd like to view it.

PUBLISH YOUR EBOOK

Whereas the last chapter focused on uploading the files to make your paperback book available for sale, this chapter will run through the same process for your ebook. Fortunately, things are much simpler on the ebook side.

UPLOADING YOUR EBOOK TO AMAZON

There are many possible places to sell your ebook, but one marketplace dwarfs the rest: Amazon.

Amazon's Kindle pioneered the ebook market, and the vast majority of ebooks are sold on Amazon today.[32] If you only upload your book to Amazon and nowhere else, that wouldn't be a problem at all in terms of reach or sales.

Unlike CreateSpace, which is an outside company that Amazon

---

32 www.forbes.com/sites/jeffbercovici/2014/02/10/amazon-vs-book-publishers-by-the-numbers/#63a05af465a3

bought to allow people to easily upload their print books, KDP (Kindle Direct Publishing) is a native part of Amazon.

KDP is simple. You upload your files, enter the information, and in less than 24 hours the book will be live.

KDP is even more intuitive than CreateSpace, so this part of the process shouldn't give you any trouble. However, we've also created a walkthrough to guide you through this process, just in case. You can download the video at bookinabox.com/resources.

For books priced between $2.99 and $9.99, Amazon pays you 70% royalties (make sure to select the 70% royalty option, or they may default to 35%). For books priced outside of that range, your only option will be to select the 35% royalty.

This is pretty clear. If your goal is to maximize revenue for the book, you want to make sure you're inside that window. If you're more focused on moving copies than making money, sometimes it'll make sense to price the book at $0.99 or $1.99.

There's almost no time that pricing the book above $10 makes sense for ebooks.

OTHER EBOOK RETAILERS

Despite Amazon being the big gorilla in the ebook market, there are other places. Apple's iBooks sells some copies, as do Nook, Kobo, and other ebook retailers.

The standard way to upload your book to all of these retailers is to go through them all one at a time.

For example, to get your book on iBooks, you'll need to sign up for iTunes Connect, download an app call iTunes Producer, and upload the book that way. Each retailer has their own process.

We're not going to walk through instructions on how to upload to each of these platforms, simply because their walkthroughs are all pretty good:

* iBooks[33]
* Kobo[34]
* Nook[35]

There is an even simpler way: Book Baby.[36]

Book Baby is an ebook distributor. They charge a flat fee of $299 to convert your manuscripts into ebook format, and then distribute your book to over 60 online retailers.

If you'd like to get your ebook into other retailers beyond just Amazon, they're the easy choice.

You upload to one place, your royalties are paid out from one

33 http://www.apple.com/ibooks/

34 http://www.kobobooks.com/

35 http://www.barnesandnoble.com/b/nook-books/_/N-8qa

36 http://bookbaby.com

place, and you're able to see all the data on how many sales are coming where.

The amount of time and energy it'll save you is easily worth it, and we recommend them to you.

CONCLUSION: IT'S TIME TO FINALLY PUBLISH YOUR BOOK

We know this can seem a little bit overwhelming at first. There is a very simple way to make it easy:

Go step by step, work the process in front of you and nothing else, and you'll eventually finish.

We created this process to make it simple and easy, as long as **you just do the work**.

You never have to wonder what the next step or piece of process is—it's right there in front of you. You just put one foot in front of the other, each day, until you are done.

You don't have to wonder if this will work. We know this process works. It has worked for hundreds of authors.

That being said, each time we have done it, we've been the ones implementing it. Our authors only have to spend about 15 to 20 hours on the phone and we do the rest of the work.

It is possible that this book either fails to explain some part of the process well or in some way misguides an author who is doing this without our direct assistance.

If at any point in the course of working this process you get stuck or find something in the book that doesn't make sense, or your just need help—come ask us. We are happy to help.

In fact, every time you ask us for help, it's a blessing to us. It helps us see if there is something we aren't communicating well, and let's us figure out if we need to improve the process, or our communication of the process.

So please ask anything you want by emailing us: help@bookinabox.com

ABOUT THE AUTHORS

TUCKER MAX

Tucker Max is the co-founder and Chairman of Book In A Box. He has written three #1 *New York Times* Best Sellers, which have sold over 3 million copies worldwide. He is credited with being the originator of the literary genre, "fratire," and is only the third writer (after Malcolm Gladwell and Michael Lewis) to ever have three books on the *New York Times* Nonfiction Best Seller List at one time.

He co-wrote and produced the movie based on his life/book, both titled *I Hope They Serve Beer In Hell*. He was nominated to the Time Magazine 100 Most Influential List in 2009.

He received his BA from the University of Chicago in 1998, and his JD from Duke Law School in 2001. He currently lives in Austin, Texas, with his wife Veronica and son Bishop.

ZACH OBRONT

Zach Obront is the co-founder of Book In A Box, a new type of publishing company focused on allowing busy experts with important messages to share to create their book without the usual barriers. Prior to Book In A Box, he ran Lioncrest Publishing and BookPop Book Marketing.

As an expert in the changing publishing industry, he's spoken to crowds at Harvard, Yale, Google, and Adobe, and has worked directly with hundreds of authors to professionally publish and promote their books, reaching hundreds of thousands of readers in the process.

Zach currently lives in Austin, TX, where he enjoys playing volleyball and eating the world's best barbecue.